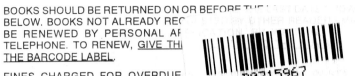

D0715967

Leabharlanna Poiblí Bárdas Atha Cliath
Dublin Corporation Public Libraries

Charleville Mall Branch   Tel. 8749619

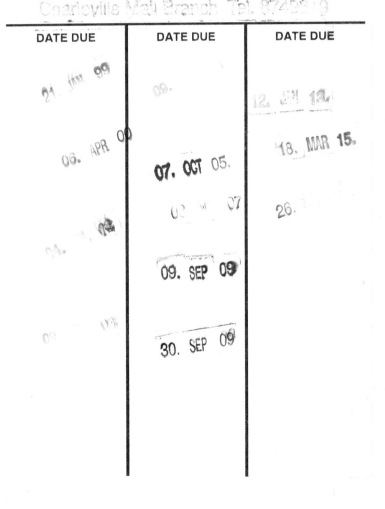

POBLACHT NA H EIREANN.

THE PROVISIONAL GOVERNMENT
OF THE

IRISH REPUBLIC
TO THE PEOPLE OF IRELAND.

IRISHMEN AND IRISHWOMEN : In the name of God and of the dead generations from which she receives her old tradition of nationhood, Ireland, through us, summons her children to her flag and strikes for her freedom.

Having organised and trained her manhood through her secret revolutionary organisation, the Irish Republican Brotherhood, and through her open military organisations, the Irish Volunteers and the Irish Citizen Army, having patiently perfected her discipline, having resolutely waited for the right moment to reveal itself, she now seizes that moment, and, supported by her exiled children in America and by gallant allies in Europe, but relying in the first on her own strength, she strikes in full confidence of victory.

We declare the right of the people of Ireland to the ownership of Ireland, and to the unfettered control of Irish destinies, to be sovereign and indefeasible. The long usurpation of that right by a foreign people and government has not extinguished the right, nor can it ever be extinguished except by the destruction of the Irish people. In every generation the Irish people have asserted their right to national freedom and sovereignty : six times during the past three hundred years they have asserted it in arms. Standing on that fundamental right and again asserting it in arms in the face of the world, we hereby proclaim the Irish Republic as a Sovereign Independent State, and we pledge our lives and the lives of our comrades-in-arms to the cause of its freedom, of its welfare, and of its exaltation among the nations.

The Irish Republic is entitled to, and hereby claims, the allegiance of every Irishman and Irishwoman. The Republic guarantees religious and civil liberty, equal rights and equal opportunities to all its citizens, and declares its resolve to pursue the happiness and prosperity of the whole nation and of all its parts, cherishing all the children of the nation equally, and oblivious of the differences carefully fostered by an alien government, which have divided a minority from the majority in the past.

Until our arms have brought the opportune moment for the establishment of a permanent National Government, representative of the whole people of Ireland and elected by the suffrages of all her men and women, the Provisional Government, hereby constituted, will administer the civil and military affairs of the Republic in trust for the people.

We place the cause of the Irish Republic under the protection of the Most High God, Whose blessing we invoke upon our arms, and we pray that no one who serves that cause will dishonour it by cowardice, inhumanity, or rapine. In this supreme hour the Irish nation must, by its valour and discipline and by the readiness of its children to sacrifice themselves for the common good, prove itself worthy of the august destiny to which it is called.

Signed on Behalf of the Provisional Government,

THOMAS J. CLARKE.

SEAN Mac DIARMADA,	THOMAS MacDONAGH,
P. H. PEARSE,	EAMONN CEANNT,
JAMES CONNOLLY.	JOSEPH PLUNKETT.

IRISH REBELLIONS

1798–1916

An Illustrated History

Helen Litton

Picture Research: Peter Costello

WOLFHOUND PRESS
& in the US and Canada
The Irish American Book Company

First published in 1998 by
Wolfhound Press Ltd
68 Mountjoy Square
Dublin 1, Ireland
Tel: (353-1) 874 0354
Fax: (353-1) 872 0207

Published in the US and Canada by
The Irish American Book Company
6309 Monarch Park Place
Niwot, Colorado 80503, USA
Tel: (303) 652-2710; Fax: (303) 652-2689

Wolfhound Press receives financial assistance from the Arts Council/ An Chomhairle Ealaíon, Dublin, Ireland.

British Library Cataloguing in Publication Data
A catalogue record for this book is available from the British Library.

ISBN 0-86327-634-2

10 9 8 7 6 5 4 3 2 1

Cover Painting: The Execution of Robert Emmet outside St Catherine's Church, Dublin, in 1803; with contemporary engraving of battle in Wexford Town during the 1798 Rebellion. Courtesy Pat Cooke, Kilmainham Museum; private collection.
Cover Design: Slick Fish Design, Dublin
Typesetting: Wolfhound Press
Printed in the Republic of Ireland by Colour Books, Dublin.

PREFACE

This book is a very brisk survey of the most well-known rebellions of Irish history, from the United Irishmen of 1798 to the Irish Volunteers of 1916.

From the time that Britain first began to take an interest in the country on her western side, the history of the two islands has been one of constant struggle and misunderstanding. However, the most important developments are often those that take place slowly and quietly, taking years to come to maturity. Perhaps some of these possibilities were sidetracked or derailed completely by sudden eruptions of violence; or perhaps these eruptions helped to encourage something which would otherwise have failed. Readers can make up their own minds.

Irish Rebellions: An Illustrated History begins with 1798, as its bicentenary is being commemorated in 1998. This rising, and the others dealt with here, were manifestations of a groundswell of movement for civil and religious rights, and national independence, in a way not true of earlier uprisings.

The Nine Years' War in the time of Queen Elizabeth I, spearheaded by Hugh O'Neill, Earl of Tyrone, and Hugh O'Donnell, Earl of Tyrconnell, was a final, despairing effort to hold onto ancestral lands, and prevent the inexorable movement of Tudor forces throughout Ireland. It ended when the chiefs of Ireland sailed away to Spain in 1607 (the 'Flight of the Earls'), leaving their people behind in a ravaged countryside to face starvation and brutality. It is unlikely that these leaders were thinking in 'nationalistic' terms; each was fighting for his own heritage, and to go back to the old ways.

The Tudor system of plantations — that is, 'planting' Protestant settlers from Britain in confiscated areas of Ireland — continued throughout the seventeenth century. Any kind of rebellion simply provided the authorities with more excuses for confiscation, a sort of fig-leaf to conceal greed. The tensions created by placing small groups of vulnerable settlers among large numbers of dispossessed natives often led to brutal and despairing outbreaks, instantly punished by the arrival of troops. One of these was the Rising of 1641, planned in Ulster by members of the dispossessed noble Gaelic families. Rebels plundered Dundalk, Newry, Carrickmacross and other towns. Many settler families were killed or injured, and rumours of mass slaughters spread wildly. The Rising spread to Connaught and Leinster, and as far as Limerick and Tipperary, but had been defeated by spring of 1642, although the Confederate War which followed lasted until 1644. This rising went down in Protestant mythology as an example of what Catholics were capable of if they were not strictly controlled (or, preferably, exterminated). But there was very little in the way of central co-ordination, or national aim, to begin with.

This book may help to demonstrate how successful later leaders were, either in imposing any kind of central command, or in developing a universally supported aim through their activities.

My grateful thanks are due to Peter Costello, for the picture research, and to Wolfhound Press, for giving me the opportunity to explore these events.

Helen Litton
1998

1

THE REBELLION OF 1798

The train of explosive which led to the rebellion of 1798 was laid by the American War of Independence (1775–83), and the fuse was lit by the French Revolution of 1789. Eighteenth-century western Europe was a ferment of new ideas about the Rights of Man, democracy and republicanism, and a growing resentment of tyranny and royalism.

In Ireland, these ideas were slow to take root, largely because there was no system of universal education. Those who were first attracted by them were educated middle-class gentlemen, including some members of the Irish Parliament. Many of those initially involved in the United Irish movement were Presbyterians, belonging to a form of Protestantism different from the dominant church (the Church of Ireland). They had suffered under Penal Laws in the same way as Catholics, although to a lesser extent.

In 1793, a Catholic Relief Act gave Catholics some legal freedoms, but not enough. New thinking about the equality of all mankind in the sight of God, and the offensiveness of bigotry and prejudice on the grounds of religion, inspired the ultimate leaders of the 1798 rebellion to work for a freer and more equal society. This would mean removing the king as the head of the state, and they accepted that this could be done only by force.

Roots of the United Irishmen

The Volunteers, a people's militia, had been formed in 1778 to defend Ireland against possible invasion by France while Britain was fighting the American War of Independence. They gradually developed in a political direction, and supported the principle that the Irish Parliament should be fully independent of the British Parliament. At that time, laws passed in the Irish Parliament had to be ratified in England, and could be overturned there. Some Irish MPs were growing impatient with this lack of autonomy. However, there was also a parallel movement among other MPs towards even closer links with England, with one parliament for both countries.

A huge Volunteer Convention was held at Dungannon, Co. Tyrone, in 1782, at which time the Volunteers were said to number 80,000. Intense pressure was brought on the government, and the Irish Parliament was allowed to pass a 'Declaration of Independence'. Now the Irish Parliament had a larger degree of independent function, but it was still executively dependent on Britain, and any freedom of movement was more apparent than real. It was known as 'Grattan's Parliament', after Henry Grattan, its most prominent member, and lasted until 1800, when the Act of Union swept it away completely.

Meanwhile, the Volunteer companies had gradually disbanded, unwilling to take the final step of physically attacking the institutions of the State.

In 1782 a Relief Act gave Catholics full rights to own land and property, and the need for resistance seemed even less urgent. However, a remnant of the Volunteers had formed a secret radical committee in Belfast, trying to get support for revolutionary ideas.

These men were attracted by an anonymous pamphlet called *An Argument on behalf of the Catholics of Ireland.* This urged Protestants and Catholics to join together, in mutual respect and esteem, to fight for the cause of Irish independence. Samuel Neilson, a leader of the Belfast committee, contacted the author of this paper, a young Protestant called Theobald Wolfe Tone, through a mutual friend, Thomas Russell, another radical.

The young Wolfe Tone in his Irish Volunteer uniform, before he went to France.
Dr Madden's The United Irishmen.

Tone was a member of the Catholic Committee, a group which worked in Dublin for civil rights for Catholics, but he was moving away from its conservative views towards a more extreme republicanism. He is described as having 'a hatchet face, a long aquiline nose, rather handsome and genteel-looking, with lank, straight hair combed down on his sickly red cheek'. A student of law, he had married at twenty-two, but had not settled to a career.

Tone came to Belfast to meet Neilson and his group, and the Belfast Society of United Irishmen was formed. It held its first public meeting on 18 October 1791. Returning to Dublin, Tone established another branch of the United Irishmen with James 'Napper' Tandy, an ex-Volunteer. The Society started out as more

. . . We have agreed to form an association, to be called 'THE SOCIETY OF UNITED IRISHMEN'. And we do pledge ourselves to our country, and mutually to each other, that we will steadily support, and endeavour, by all due means, to carry into effect, the following resolutions:

First, Resolved, That the weight of English influence in the Government of this country is so great, as to require a cordial union among ALL THE PEOPLE OF IRELAND, to maintain that balance which is essential to the preservation of our liberties, and the extension of our commerce.

Second, That the sole constitutional mode by which this influence can be opposed, is by a complete and radical reform of the representation of the people in Parliament.

Third, That no reform is practicable, efficacious, or just, which shall not include Irishmen of every *religious* persuasion.

Satisfied, as we are, that the internecine divisions among Irishmen have too often given encouragement and impunity to profligate, audacious, and corrupt Administrations, in measures which, but for these divisions, they durst not have attempted; we submit our resolutions to the nation, as the basis of our political faith.

THEOBALD WOLFE TONE, Belfast, October 1791

of a debating society than anything else, and did not become a secret society until 1794. Its members made an 'affirmation', instead of swearing an oath. Other founder-members included Dr William Drennan, Beauchamp Bagenal Harvey (a Wexford land-owner), and the brothers Henry and John Sheares, one of whom was a barrister. All of these were Protestants.

Agrarian Struggle

In the Irish countryside, because of a desperately unfair and unequal system of land ownership, there was a long tradition of so-called 'agrarian agitation'. Demonstrations, often followed by riots, called for rights of land ownership, death to landlords, fair rents and so on. These movements occasionally developed into small, badly organised secret societies, whose main aim seemed to be the assault and intimidation of undefended neighbours and people no better off than themselves.

Such a group was the 'Defenders', a widely spread Catholic organisation which raided wealthy homes for weapons and money. Although Defenders took an oath to support revolutionary principles, they were also highly sectarian, often fighting viciously with equally sectarian Protestant groups such as the Peep O'Day Boys or, later, members of the Orange Order (founded in 1795). The Defenders had no centralised organisation, and were put down easily, often with the utmost brutality, by government troops. Large numbers of them were hanged or transported, and the United Irishmen, observing this growing anarchy, were confirmed in their belief that the whole system of society had to change.

Opportunities

In 1793, England and France went to war. The French were interested in supporting an Irish rebellion to keep the English engaged on two fronts at once, and began to send out feelers to Republican sympathisers in Ireland. Meanwhile Wolfe Tone had been detected in treasonable activity in Dublin, and had left Ireland for America. The Society of United Irishmen was suddenly banned, although its activities had been strictly legal. In response, Samuel Neilson established a new, secret, oath-bound society, keeping the old name, but changing its objectives towards a physical rebellion.

The French war went badly for England at first. Worried about the threat of radical societies in Ireland and their French contacts, the government passed an Insurrection Act in March 1796. The Defenders, who were growing in numbers and strength and becoming more organised, now responded to contacts from the Society of United Irishmen, and the two groups finally came together under the one oath. This was an unlikely combination. The Defenders were often sectarian in motivation, but the United Irishmen were supposed to stand for 'liberty, equality and fraternity', with no room for religious quarrels.

Wolfe Tone went to France in 1796, and made contact with the ruling post-revolution Directory. Plans were laid for definite military help to be sent to Ireland, under General Hoche. The French had already been in contact with Lord Edward Fitzgerald and Arthur O'Connor, both members of the Irish Parliament, who were close to the United Irishmen's society, although they had not joined it. It seems clear that the French were given an inflated impression of Ireland's readiness for revolution — thousands of patriots would spring up to fling the British out, and were only waiting for their brave French brothers to join them. In reality, nothing like this level of organisation existed.

Hoche's expedition consisted of 14,000 troops in 43 ships. It set sail in December 1796, accompanied by Wolfe Tone, who was in high spirits at the prospect of revolutionary action at last. Five days later, after a stormy crossing during which nine ships either sank or turned back, the fleet arrived at Bantry Bay, in Co. Cork. During the night, twenty of the ships were blown out to sea again by strong gales, and heavy snow fell. Unfortunately, one of the

Lord Edward Fitzgerald, from a nineteenth-century woodcut.
Central Catholic Library.

ships which had failed to arrive at all was the one containing General Hoche, so the remaining small number of troops did not even have a commander.

The only defensive forces immediately available to the authorities in Ireland were the Galway militia, 400 men or so.

These were mobilised, but found no enemy to fight. The storms and gales had increased, and Admiral Bouvet had ordered his ships out to sea again, fearing they would be wrecked on the shore. Here they set sail once again for France. Those few French who had landed, briefly, found that the local peasantry, while welcoming, showed no signs whatsoever of enthusiastically taking arms side by side with them, but concentrated on looking after the Galway militia. One contemporary letter says that the Cork Irish thought that the French had been invited to Ireland by Northern Protestants. This to them meant the vicious sectarianism of the Peep O'Day Boys, and they feared the French had come to drive them from their homes.

However much of a failure this expedition had been, it galvanised the United Irishmen and the Defenders. They had not really believed that the French would support them to such an extent, but here was the proof. Membership swelled daily, proper plans were laid, weapons were collected. Firearms were always going to be scarce, so the most important weapon was the pike. Cheaply made by local blacksmiths and set on poles, pikes were to become symbolic of the 1798 Rebellion. Another symbol was the tightly cropped hair, a sign of revolutionary sympathies; supporters were called 'croppies'.

However, problems that had been superficially solved still remained deeply buried, waiting to undermine the motley alliance. As Bardon describes it: 'The Defenders ... sought wholesale land confiscation. The bourgeois leaders had in mind a government similar to the French Directory with themselves in charge — major social upheaval was not part of their agenda. The Presbyterian farmers east of the Bann ... were the true democrats seeking popular parliamentary government, freedom of conscience and expression, and equality before the law.'

These disparate forces could not work together for long. By the time rebellion finally broke out, in 1798, the United Irishmen consisted of a Catholic core, under Protestant leaders. They would be facing yeomanry and militia who were mostly Irish, partly Catholic, but largely strongly sectarian Protestants.

Reign of Terror

The British authorities were equally shocked by the French invasion attempt. Dublin Castle decided that a reign of terror was the only answer, and authorised Lieutenant-General Gerard Lake to run this campaign. Concentrating on Ulster, as the spearhead of possible revolution, he proclaimed martial law in Belfast in early 1797. His troops seized enormous numbers of pikes and firearms. Hundreds of prisoners were taken in Ulster, and the militia flogged and terrorised hundreds more. Fifty or so were executed. The United Irishmen had been more strongly organised in Ulster than elsewhere, but by the end of 1797 this was no longer the case.

In Dublin, a government spy named Thomas Reynolds infiltrated the Leinster Directory of the United Irishmen. He passed on details of the planned rising, and the leaders were arrested in March 1798, including Thomas Addis Emmet, a barrister; Oliver Bond, a wool merchant; and W.J. MacNeven, the only Catholic on the Executive. Lord Edward Fitzgerald, a young aristocrat who had been a British army officer, had finally joined the United Irishmen, along with Arthur O'Connor, and acted as military organiser. He initially managed to escape, but was badly wounded in a struggle later on, and died in prison of septicaemia. His sister Lucy wrote to Thomas Paine, highly influential author of *The Rights of Man*, 'Citizen, although he was unsuccessful in the glorious attempt of liberating his country from slavery, still he was not unworthy of the lesson you taught him'.

The government decided that the only way to prevent a rebellion was to blanket the country with a campaign of activities similar to that of General Lake in Ulster. The militia (most of them, it should be remembered, Irish themselves) were given free rein to terrorise the population, and it is to this period that the frightful tales of flogging, pitch-capping and half-hanging belong. Hundreds of people died in agony, or survived in a crippled condition. Families began to sleep in the fields for safety, terrified that theirs would be the next house to be broken into and ravaged.

The arrest of Lord Edward Fitzgerald (May 1798). Engraving by George Cruikshank from Maxwell's History of the Irish Rebellion of 1798. *Mansell Collection, Katz Picture Library.*

Rebellion

Despite the State's worst efforts, and the wholesale arrest of the most prominent leaders, rebellion did break out in the south of the country in May and June 1798. The population was being driven to a pitch of despair, and the remaining leaders risked all on one cast. Since the central committee had been shattered, there was very little co-ordination between different areas; communications were almost impossible. Frantic efforts were made to substitute inexperienced leaders, and make new strategy on the spot. The two Sheares brothers, who had escaped the earlier searches, took over command in Leinster, but were themselves arrested several weeks later.

The area most actively involved in the rising of 1798 was Co. Wexford, but events took place elsewhere to a lesser extent, including counties Antrim and Down in Ulster.

UNITE AND BE FREE

Tune, '*The Green Cockade*'

Ye lovers of UNION, of ev'ry degree,
No matter what Trade or Religion ye be,
The right-hand of friendship to you I'll extend,
And hope for your pardon if I should offend.

For the Rights of Man let us always be,
And Unite in the cause that will make us Free,
Till oppression and tyranny's banish'd the land,
We'll fight for our country with heart and hand.

I'm slave to no sect, and from bigotry free,
And follow what conscience still dictates to me;
All men are my brethren who'r ready to lend
Their aid to the country, and hand to a friend.

For the Rights of Man, etc.

Let the creatures of kings, and the dupes of a priest,
Bow down to a *bauble*, or worship a beast —
Shall an impious prelate, a statesman, or prince,
Set marks to our reason, or bounds to our sense?

For the Rights of Man, etc.

'Divide then and conquer' — the maxim of knaves,
Who have practis'd it long on a nation of slaves —
But the bright Star of Reason will soon let them see
That *Hibernians* were made to UNITE AND BE FREE.

For the Rights of Man, etc.

Paddy's Resource, Belfast, 1795

Wexford

Wexford was a prosperous county, with a large Protestant minority, and a strong liberal tradition. The stirrings of republicanism appealed to the social level above the peasantry — the farmers and artisans, merchants and teachers — and particularly to the young. Unrest had been growing in the county throughout 1797, following the French retreat, and was fuelled by a fall in grain prices, and by defeats of Liberal candidates in the general election of that year.

By the end of the year, sixteen Wexford parishes were said to be in a state of rebellion. Martial law was declared in April 1798, and followed by the usual round of arrests, tortures and arms searches. The North Cork militia, who were to become a byword for brutality, brought with them to Wexford an officers' Orange Lodge, adding to sectarian tensions.

The Dublin leadership had planned the outbreak of rebellion for 23 May 1798. Local units were to attack local government forces, and Dublin would be taken over by the Leinster Directory. However, the arrests of the leaders threw everything into confusion; government troops managed to hold Dublin, and local units, rising individually on 23 May, were easily defeated. By 25 May, rebellion had broken out only in Wicklow, Carlow, Kildare and Meath.

Showing as they rushed into Tullow street [Carlow], with that vain confidence which is commonly followed by disappointment, that the town was their own, they received so destructive a fire from the garrison, that they recoiled and endeavoured to retreat; but finding their flight intercepted, numbers took refuge in the houses, where they found a miserable exit, these being immediately fired by the soldiery. About eight houses were consumed in this conflagration, and for some days the roasted remains of unhappy men were falling down the chimneys in which they had perished.

REV. JAMES GORDON
History of the Rebellion in Ireland in the Year 1798

Eight scenes from the History of the Irish Rebellion of 1798, *published in 1799*

Above: *The French in Bantry Bay, during the failed expedition in December 1796.*

p. 20, top: *Rebel chiefs taken in cave.*

p. 20, bottom: *Irish Yeomanry dispersing gang of Irish murderers.*

p. 21, top: *The Battle of New Ross, which the rebels failed to hold, 5 June 1798.*

p. 21, bottom: *King's soldiers entering Wexford, 21 June 1798.*

p. 22–3: *The Battle of Vinegar Hill.*

p. 24, top: *The Battle of Ballinamuck, 7 September 1798.*

p. 24, bottom: *Landing the prisoners, who included Wolfe Tone, at Lough Swilly, November 1798.*

The units in Wexford were uncertain what to do. As they hesitated, stories began to reach them of brutal counterattacks on revolutionaries in Carlow and Kildare. One of the Wexford leaders, Anthony Perry, a Protestant strong farmer, was arrested and tortured, but refused to give any information. His immediate lieutenants panicked when they heard of his arrest, and went into hiding, so the northern baronies of Wexford remained dormant.

Other Wexford leaders whose names we know include George Sparks, another Protestant farmer; Matthew Keogh, a Protestant merchant; Beauchamp Bagenal Harvey; numerous Catholic farmers, and several Catholic priests. However, the rebellion was opposed by the local Catholic bishop and most of the priests, and many important Catholic laymen also opposed it. Loyalist Catholics and Protestants joined the yeomanry, a civilian militia, in large numbers, as the threat of rebellion increased, and were responsible for many arrests in early May.

On 26 May the Wexford United Irishmen began to move. Perry had finally broken under torture, and named several leaders who were immediately arrested, such as Harvey and Keogh. However, units proceeded as planned, their first aim being to get hold of weapons. Large houses were targeted — the homes of landlords and magistrates — and many of the raids were successful. Groups began to gather at such landmarks as Oulart Hill, and camps were set up.

An attack on Oulart Hill by the North Cork militia was driven off by the rebels, and they were encouraged by this to march on Enniscorthy. They took the town and burnt it, setting up camp nearby at Vinegar Hill, and later captured the town of Wexford itself when its garrison withdrew.

The rebels by and large were undisciplined, and local activities depended on individual leaders, and whether they were brutal or compassionate, or had more than nominal control. On Vinegar Hill, for example, about thirty-five Protestant prisoners were executed by the rebels for no particular reason. Nor were they disciplined in battle, relying on fierce rushes to startle their opponents. They had little or no military training.

Mr Perry of Inch, a protestant gentleman, was seized on and brought a prisoner to Gorey, guarded by the North Cork Militia; one of whom, the noted sergeant, nicknamed *Tom the devil* ... cut off the hair of his head very closely, cut the sign of the cross from the front to the back, and transversely from ear to ear, still closer; and probably a pitched cap not being in readiness, gun powder was mixed through the hair, which was then set on fire, and the shocking process repeated, until every atom of hair that remained could be easily pulled out by the roots; and still a burning candle was continually applied, until the entire was completely singed away, and the head left totally and miserably blistered!

EDWARD HAY, *History of the Insurrection of 1798*

Entering Wexford, the rebels freed the imprisoned Harvey and made him commander-in-chief. Keogh, also freed, was put in charge of Wexford itself. These two tried to put some order on the situation and to organise the rebel force, by now numbering about 16,000. A column of men was sent to attack the town of New Ross, while another moved north to Bunclody. A third part of the force moved towards Dublin, hoping to take Arklow and Gorey on the way.

In hindsight, it seems to us obvious that these successes were going to be short-lived, and that no real overthrow of society was taking place. However, real panic developed among those living through this time of horror. Many Protestants, convinced that this was a Catholic uprising and that they would be slaughtered, pleaded with priests to baptise them as Catholics, and some could be seen at Mass beating their breasts with exaggerated gestures. The wearing of green emblems or garments became essential to avoid accusations of disloyalty, and many well-bred ladies used their needleworking skills to make banners for the rebel troops.

The recovery of Charles Davis of Enniscorthy, a glazier, was extraordinary. After having remained four days concealed in the sink of a privy, during which time he had no other sustenance than the raw body of a cock, which had by accident alighted on the seat, he fled from this loathsome abode, but was taken at some distance from the town, brought to Vinegar-hill, shot thro' the body and one of his arms, violently struck in several parts of the head with thrusts of a pike, which, however, penetrated not into the brain, and thrown into a grave on his back, with a heap of earth and stones over him. His faithful dog, having scraped away the covering from his face, and cleansed it by licking the blood, he returned to life after an interment of twelve hours, dreaming that pikemen were proceeding to stab him, and pronouncing the name of Father Roach, by whose interposition he hoped to be released. Some superstitious persons hearing the name, and imagining the man to have been revivified by the favour of Heaven, in order that he might receive salvation from the priest, by becoming a catholic, before final departure, took him from the grave to a house, and treated him with such kind attention that he recovered, and is now living in apparently perfect health.

REV. JAMES GORDON
History of the Rebellion in Ireland in the Year 1798

Edward Hay, in his later history of the rebellion, pointed out that these ladies conveniently managed to forget their collaboration once the danger had passed.

The rebel attack on New Ross took place on 5 June. It lasted for thirteen hours, but the rebels at last had to withdraw with heavy losses. One of the worst atrocities of the rebellion then took place, when 200 prisoners held by the rebels were burnt to death in a barn at Scullabogue. Those fleeing from New Ross to Scullabogue must have aroused the passions of the rebel guards, because there was no reason to kill these prisoners, many of them women and children. Appalled by the massacre, Harvey forbade any further deaths or 'executions', thus saving the lives of some prisoners held at Gorey.

Fr Murphy, rebel priest of Boulavogue, based on a contemporary drawing, now lost. Central Catholic Library.

The rebels heading for Dublin fought and won a skirmish at Tubberneering, under Fr Roche. They captured several cannon, and deployed them at Arklow. Here, however, they were beaten off despite a vigorous assault.

Meanwhile the forces heading for Bunclody, under Fr Kearns, won the town from the militia, but plundered the wine-shops to such an extent that they could not resist the counterattack which followed. Many rebels died in that attack.

*Croppy Boy memorial in Enniscorthy, one of a number erected around 1898
to mark the centenary of the rebellion.
Photo courtesy P.J. Browne.*

The runaways, declaring that the royal army in Ross were shooting all the prisoners, and butchering the catholics who had fallen into their hands, feigned an order from Harvey for the execution of those at Scullabogue. This order, which Harvey, himself a protestant and a man of humanity, was utterly incapable of giving, Murphy is said to have resisted — but his resistance was vain. Thirty-seven were shot and piked at the hall-door; and the rest, a hundred and eighty-four in number, crammed into a barn, were burned alive — the roof being fired, and straw thrown into the flames to feed the conflagration.... A few Romanists, according to some accounts fifteen in number, one of whom was Father Shallow's clerk, had been, partly by mistake or inadvertence, partly from obnoxious circumstances in the unfortunate objects, inclosed in the barn with the protestants, and by the precipitancy of the murderers shared the same fate.

REV. JAMES GORDON
History of the Rebellion in Ireland in the Year 1798

In Wexford, Harvey was deposed as commander-in-chief, accused of weakness, and the position was given to Fr Roche. Harvey despaired of the situation: 'God knows where the business will end, but end how it will the good men of both parties will inevitably be ruined'. It became obvious that the rebels were not capable of following through their successes, and that the strength of the government forces would finally overwhelm them. Another massacre took place at Wexford Bridge; about a hundred Protestant prisoners were piked or shot, and thrown into the river. The rebels then left the town, and consolidated their forces at Vinegar Hill.

Here the final battle took place, on 21 June. The government troops were commanded by General Lake. Having shattered the rebel forces with cannon-fire, they stormed the summit of the hill. A large number of rebels managed to escape, but the Wexford rebellion was essentially over. Those who escaped divided into roving bands, desperately trying to escape the yeomanry and militia which covered the countryside. Many ended up in the hills

... a man of the name of George Sparrow, a butcher from Enniscorthy, chased by the people through the streets, ran up to me and clasped me round the body, imploring protection — beseeching I might save him. I instantly endeavoured as much as in my power to give him succour, and to defend him by extending my arms and body over him, while swords and pikes were pointed and brandished for his destruction; but my endeavours proving ineffectual, and rather dangerous to myself, and the unfortunate man perceiving I could not afford the protection I intended, burst from me, and while I lay prostrate in the street, occasioned by his effort to get off, he had not run many yards when he was deprived of existence.

EDWARD HAY, *History of the Rebellion of 1798*

of Co. Wicklow, under the leadership of Michael Dwyer (who surrendered only in 1803) and Joseph Holt. In later years, it was said that the unmarked graves of 1798 rebels could be identified by the wheat sprouting from the ground: they had carried it in their pockets for food.

Massacre at Wexford Bridge

The victims were conducted in successive parcels, of from ten to twenty, with horrible solemnity — each parcel surrounded by its guard of butchers, and preceded by a black flag marked with a white cross, to the place of execution, where they were variously put to death one after another, but mostly each by four men at once, who, standing two before and two behind the victim, thrust their pikes into the body, and raising it from the ground, held it suspended, writhing with pain, while any signs of life appeared.... As an entertaining spectacle, in fact, it seems to have been regarded by a multitude of wretches, the greater part women, assembled to behold it, who rent the air with shouts of exultation on the arrival of each fresh parcel of victims at the fatal spot.

REV. JAMES GORDON
History of the Rebellion in Ireland in the Year 1798

In one point I think we must allow some praise to the rebels. Amid all their atrocities the chastity of the fair sex was respected. I have not been able to ascertain one instance to the contrary in the county of Wexford, though many beautiful young women were absolutely within their power.... They were everywhere accompanied by great numbers of women of their own party who, in the general dissolution of regular government, and the joy of imagined victory, were perhaps less scrupulous than at other times of their favours. The want of such an accompaniment to the royal troops may in some degree account for an opposite behaviour in them to the female peasantry, on their entering into the country at the retreat of the rebels, many of whose female relatives, promiscuously with others, suffered in respect of chastity, some also with respect to health, by their constrained acquaintance with the soldiery.

REV. JAMES GORDON
History of the Rebellion in Ireland in the Year 1798

Rebellion in the North

The United Irishmen in Ulster had been demoralised by General Lake's campaign and the arrests of most of the leaders. In the event, small risings took place in counties Antrim and Down, but there was no co-ordination between them. Henry Joy McCracken, who had founded the Belfast United Irishmen with Neilson, Tone and Thomas Russell in 1791, took over as commander-in-chief at the last minute, but his forces were defeated in an attempt to capture Antrim town.

Three days after this, on 12 June, the rebels in Co. Down began operations under Henry Monro, a draper. They fought a fierce battle at Ballinahinch, but were heavily defeated. Minor skirmishes also took place, but the battle of Ballinahinch was in effect the end of the rebellion in Ulster. McCracken and Monro were executed. It is probable that religious differences accounted for the failure in Ulster; news of the massacres perpetrated by rebel troops in Wexford must have reached the north before the rising began, and would have rekindled memories of the Catholic rising of 1641, when many Protestants had been slaughtered.

THE MEMORY OF THE DEAD

Who fears to speak of Ninety-Eight? Who blushes at the name?
When cowards mock the patriot's fate, Who hangs his head for shame?
He's all a knave or half a slave Who slights his country thus,
But a true man, like you, man, Will fill your glass with us!
(Repeat last two lines)

We drink the mem'ry of the brave, The faithful and the few.
Some lie far off beyond the wave, Some sleep in Ireland, too.
All, all are gone, but still lives on The fame of those who died.
All true men, like you, men, Remember them with pride.

Some on the shores of distant lands Their weary hearts have laid,
And by the stranger's heedless hands Their lonely graves were made;
But tho' their clay be far away, Beyond the Atlantic foam,
In true men, like you, men, Their spirit's still at home.

They rose in dark and evil days To right their native land;
They kindled here a living blaze That nothing shall withstand.
Alas! that might can vanquish right — They fell and passed away;
But true men, like you, men, Are plenty here today.

The dust of some is Irish earth, Among their own they rest;
And that same land that gave them birth Has caught them to her breast;
And we will pray that from their clay Full many a race may start
Of true men, like you, men, To act as brave a part.

Then here's their memory! may it be For us a guiding light,
To cheer our strife for liberty, And teach us to unite:
Tho' good and ill be Ireland's still, Though sad as theirs your fate,
And true men be you, men, Like those of Ninety-Eight!

JOHN KELLS INGRAM (1823–1907)

Aftermath

Some of the most brutal events of the 1798 rebellion took place in the 'mopping-up' operation which followed, when the yeomanry acted with 'violence and atrocity ... shot many after they had received protections and burned houses and committed the most unpardonable acts'. Hundreds of innocent people were butchered in their homes. Lord Cornwallis, the lord lieutenant, expressed himself horrified at the accounts he received.

> I shall mention only one act, not of what I shall call cruelty, since no pain was inflicted, but ferocity not calculated to soften the rancour of the insurgents. Some soldiers of the Ancient British regiment cut open the dead body of Father Michael Murphy, after the battle of Arklow, took out his heart, roasted the body, and oiled their boots with the grease which dripped from it!
>
> REV. JAMES GORDON
> *History of the Rebellion in Ireland in the Year 1798*

While this backlash was directed at the peasants, most of the leaders of the rebellion were tried and executed through courts martial. Harvey, Keogh and Fr Roche were hanged on Wexford Bridge, and their heads impaled on pikes. Some members of the Leinster Executive were also executed, but others were granted mercy on turning king's evidence, and were exiled.

For the rank and file, there was no mercy; hundreds were sent into forced labour in Prussia, or transported to New South Wales. Badly led and armed, many of them were victims of a cause they could not have understood, and were carried away on a tide of violence and anarchy. The leaders were aware that most of the rebels they led were not fighting for the wider causes of nationalism or republicanism. As Thomas Emmet said in his evidence: '... the object next their hearts was a redress of their grievances ... they would prefer it infinitely to a revolution and a republic'. Overall, about 2,000 loyalists and soldiers died in 1798, but the number of rebels killed, several thousand at least, remains uncertain.

A postscript to the 1798 rebellion was provided by the French, who had been persuaded by Tone to try again. Napoleon Bonaparte, now in command, was unconvinced of the importance of an Irish adventure, and was intent on sending his forces to Egypt. However, three small expeditions were provided for Ireland, one of them led by General Humbert. The other two expeditions were delayed, but Humbert set sail on 6 August, with arms and ammunition and about a thousand troops. He was accompanied by Tone, who was convinced that the Irish, further politicised by the appalling events of the previous months, would be keen to rise again, with a little encouragement.

Humbert's force landed at Killala, Co. Mayo, on 22 August, and issued a proclamation headed 'Liberty, Equality, Fraternity, Union!' Thousands of locals gathered to be given weapons and uniforms, but they were not soldiers, and could not be disciplined. Nor did they know how to use their new weapons; Humbert himself was almost killed by a carelessly discharged rifle.

Despite these disadvantages, Humbert's French and Irish army managed to defeat General Lake at Castlebar ('the Races of Castlebar'). A Provisional Government was set up under a local Catholic gentleman, John Moore. This situation lasted for a month, after which news came that Cornwallis himself was leading an army from Dublin. Attempted risings in Longford and Westmeath had been defeated. Finally, Cornwallis trapped Humbert at Ballinamuck, Co. Longford. After a brief battle, the French surrendered honourably, while the Irish were slaughtered. Killala itself was then attacked, and about 400 Irish rebels were killed.

Another part of the French expedition, accompanied by Napper Tandy, had landed in Co. Donegal, but on hearing of the battle of Ballinamuck it sailed away again. Meanwhile, Wolfe

---

Tone's Birthday

June 20. Today is my birthday — I am thirty-three years old. At that age Alexander had conquered the world; at that age Wolfe had completed his reputation, and expired in the arms of victory. Well, it is not my fault, if I am not as great a man as Alexander or Wolfe. I have as good dispositions for glory as either of them, but I labour under two small obstacles at least — want of talents and want of opportunities; neither of which, I confess, I can help. *Allons! nous verrons.* If I succeed here, I may make some noise in the world yet; and what is better, the cause to which I am devoted is so just, that I have not one circumstance to reproach myself with. I will endeavour to keep myself as pure as I can, as to the means; as to the end, it is sacred — the liberty and independence of my country first.

THEOBALD WOLFE TONE, *Journal*, 20 June 1796

Tone had been captured off Donegal, accompanying the third part of the French expedition. Tried in Dublin, he was sentenced to death, but managed to cut his own throat in prison. He died a week later. He had helped to change political attitudes in Ireland forever; the idea of a republic, and of separation from Britain, had been born. His grave in Bodenstown, Co. Kildare, is now a place of annual pilgrimage for Irish republican parties. But his ideal of complete social and religious liberty gradually faded away.

Overall, the United Irishmen had been unrealistic in hoping to overcome entrenched sectarian attitudes, bringing together in the name of liberty people who held little but contempt for one another's religious beliefs. Most of the Catholic peasants who fought were fighting for land possession, not for abstract republican ideals. Nor did the rebellion reach, for example, many Irish-speaking areas, because the leaders spread their ideas through the printed word, in English only.

Mounted officer of the rebel army in Wexford.
Wolfhound Press archive.

June 4. £200 was subscribed by the citizens, for the wives and children of the soldiers who went in pursuit of the United Irishmen at Kildare.

John Hayes, of Bilboa, committed, charged with being a United Irishman, and attempting to shoot John Lloyd, Esq., C.P. for the county.

June 6. Michael M'Swiney, charged with being a serjeant in the United Irishmen, was sentenced to 600 lashes. After having received 100 at the Main Guard, he requested to be taken down, promising to make some useful disclosures, whereupon the remainder of his sentence was remitted.

Matthew Kennedy, charged with taking arms from the house of John Evans, of Ashroe, was executed on the new bridge, and his body buried in the yard of the intended new jail.

John Moore, convicted of being a rebel captain, was hanged on the new bridge, and buried in the jail yard.

Owen Ryan, convicted of being a sworn rebel, was sentenced to receive 500 lashes, and to be sent to serve in the West Indies for life. He received 300 lashes on the new bridge.

... Persons are hourly brought in from the country, charged with aiding and abetting rebellion. The Doonas Cavalry brought in Francis McNamara, Esq., of Ardclooney, near O'Brien's Bridge, charged with holding a captain's commission in the ranks of the disaffected. Major Purdon's corps brought in twenty from Killaloe, one of whom was a Colonel M'Cormick — also a quantity of captured pike-heads. Captain Studdert's corps from Kilkishen escorted three defenders, with their pikes hung round their bodies.

June 13. Andrew Ryan, Patrick Carroll, Michael Callinan, and — Sheehy, charged with having pikes in their possession, were whipped by the drummers of the Garrison.

Daniel Hayes, to receive 800 lashes, and be transported for life.
John Collins, 100 lashes, and transportation.
James Kelly, same punishment.
Richard Kelly, 600 lashes, and transportation.
Thomas Frost, transportation for life.
William Walsh, sentenced to death, respited, and transported....

MAURICE LENIHAN, *History of Limerick*

2

THE REBELLION OF 1803

Twelve years after the rising of the United Irishmen, the Irish political landscape had changed. Ireland and Britain were united in 1800 by the Act of Union, partly driven by the events of 1798, and the Parliament of Ireland was extinguished; the Houses of Parliament in Dublin were sold to the Bank of Ireland. Executive power remained with Dublin Castle, under a lord lieutenant, but it now answered directly to London. Dublin, losing the social and political élite the Irish Parliament had attracted, entered a period of economic decline. The great houses were closed down, the wide streets no longer echoed to the passing of noble carriages. In rural areas, agrarian riots and disorder continued on a local scale, but any appetite for a rebellion had died away.

As the country settled down to the new situation, Presbyterian radical thinkers came to the conclusion that they had more to gain than to lose from the Union. They no longer suffered under legal disabilities, and could now profit from political advancement. Protestants as a whole began to be conscious of the threat of full Catholic emancipation, in a predominantly Catholic country. They saw the Union as their only protection.

In 1799, just before the Union was settled, word reached Dublin Castle that the United Irish Society had raised its head again. Thomas Addis Emmet, one of the leaders of the 1798 rising, was imprisoned in Scotland, but a younger Emmet, Robert,

Robert Emmet, a romanticised portrait of the patriot.
Central Catholic Library.

was apparently now taking up his brother's torch. Expelled from Trinity College for his political opinions, he had maintained contact with the United Irish prisoners, and became a member of the remnant of the executive which still existed.

Moves were made to arrest him, but he disappeared for some time. He was in France in 1801, but the British and French made peace in 1802, so no help could be found there. He found a place in Parisian society, where he was admired by, among others, the Comtesse D'Hausonville, who wrote: 'Energy, delicacy and tenderness are expressed in his melancholy features.... The modesty of his character, joined to a sort of habitual reserve, hid the working of his mind to the ordinary circumstances of life, but were any subject started which was deeply interesting to him, he appeared quite another man.'

Thomas Emmet, released from prison, went into exile in America, but Robert did not want to leave their parents alone in Ireland, and came home: 'I find that my father and mother have left me perfectly free to make my choice; and that they have made the sacrifices of their own wishes, and that sacrifice shows me that I must not allow myself to be carried away by personal motives.' Subterranean United Irish activity continued.

In 1802, in raids in London, thirty conspirators were arrested. Their leader was a former army officer, Colonel Despard, who had tried to unite English radicals with the United Irishmen before the 1798 rising. It was alleged that a new rising had been planned for London, but it seems more probable that efforts were being made to reopen contacts with rebels in Ireland, and to combine a joint English–Irish rising with French assistance. Despard and six others were tried and hanged.

In May 1803, Britain and France again went to war. Thomas Emmet was by now in France, and messages were sent to him from Ireland, promising a high degree of preparation for rebellion. However, the United Irish exiles in France were split among themselves, and Thomas did not have Bonaparte's ear. The hopeful rebels in Dublin asserted that anyway they were not relying on French aid, and were confident of victory through their own resources.

Plans for Rising

Robert Emmet decided to concentrate on capturing the seat of British administration in Ireland — Dublin Castle — as well as a couple of the military forts in the city. Meticulous planning was involved in preparing guns and pikes, and explosives were to be used to mine the streets, an innovative idea at the time. A notable feature of this conspiracy was its absolute secrecy; the government had suspicions, but no confirmation that anything was going on.

Emmet's explosives had been stored at several depots, and on 16 July gunpowder in a house in Patrick Street exploded accidentally, causing one fatality: 'To prevent suffocation the persons inside broke the glass and Keenan, who is since dead, cut himself so deeply by running his arm through the pane that the effusion of blood principally occasioned his death.' The authorities, alerted by this event, searched the house, but most of the weapons stored there remained hidden and were secretly removed later.

The rising had been fixed for 23 July, and Emmet decided not to postpone it, as it was likely that he would now be discovered. He expected support from the counties surrounding Dublin, as well as in Ulster, and Thomas Russell was sent to alert the men of the north. Russell, one of the leaders of 1798, had written, 'If the people are true to themselves we have an overwhelming force, if otherwise, we fail, and our lives will be sufficient sacrifice'.

This rebellion had little chance of success, although Emmet had spent £15,000 in preparations. Communications were poor, and promised forces from Wicklow never arrived. Men from Kildare did come, but decided that there were not enough weapons, and left the city. Wexfordmen waited for a signal rocket, but it was never sent up. The notion that the whole country was just waiting for Dublin to be captured before it would rise up in force seems to have been taken largely on faith; there was no real evidence for it.

The explosion in Patrick Street had left some shortages, and other equipment was lost or mislaid. According to Emmet: 'The person who had the management of the depot mixed, by accident, the slow matches that were prepared with what were not, and all our labour went for nothing. The fuses for the grenades he had also laid by, where he forgot them, and could not find in the crowd.' It is notable, however, that detailed plans had been carried through for the printing of a Proclamation, and for laced and elaborate uniforms for Emmet and his officers.

Dublin Castle was beginning to have its suspicions confirmed. Discussions in the open had been overheard by spies, and mysterious groups of men were arriving in the city. The authorities did not respond with any urgency, however, and were

Forging pikes: preparations for the insurrection in one of Emmet's workshops. Engraving by George Cruikshank. W.H. Maxwell's History of the Irish Rebellion of 1798.

severely criticised later for this. On the evening of 23 July, Emmet began to assemble his force in Thomas Street, expecting 2,000 men to meet him. Eighty turned up. Nevertheless, he distributed his Proclamation, and led his men onto the streets. Here they were gradually joined by drunken revellers and bored bystanders, and the rebel army turned into a mob.

> You are now called upon to show the world that you are competent to take your place among the nations; that you have a right to claim their recognisance of you as an independent country by the only satisfactory proof you can furnish of your capability of maintaining your independence — your wresting it from England with your own hands.... We have now, without the loss of a man, with our means of communication untouched, brought our plans to the moment when they are ripe for execution.... We therefore solemnly declare that our object is to establish a free and independent republic in Ireland. We war not against property, we war against no religious sect, we war not against past opinions or prejudices, we war against English dominion. Fully impressed with the justice of our cause, which we now put to the issue, we make our last and solemn appeal to the sword and to heaven, and as the cause of Ireland deserves to prosper, may God give us the Victory.
>
> ROBERT EMMET, Proclamation

An eyewitness describes Emmet as entering Patrick Street with fourteen or fifteen men, and shouting to the people around, 'Turn out, my boys, now is your time for Liberty. Liberty, my boys. Turn out, Turn out'. Getting no response, he fired his pistol in the air, and decided that it would be best for him to head to the Wicklow Mountains and Michael Dwyer, the 1798 rebel turned outlaw. However, the mob he left behind surrounded the carriage of Lord Kilwarden, the Lord Chief Justice, murdering him and another man with him. Emmet was greatly distressed to hear of this later.

It was obvious that the great plan had failed, and Emmet went into hiding in Wicklow with several companions. About thirty people died during the night's rioting, but that was the beginning and end of Emmet's rebellion. Outside Dublin, nothing happened, apart from a minor skirmish at Maynooth, Co. Kildare. Ulster failed to move at all. Emmet was finally arrested on 25 August. Russell was also arrested, and was among the twenty-two rebels executed. A total of about 3,000 suspected rebels were imprisoned. In December of 1803, Michael Dwyer finally surrendered in Wicklow, and his band of outlaws gave themselves up.

> Oh! breathe not his name, let it sleep in the shade,
> Where cold and unhonoured his relics are laid;
> Sad, silent and dark be the tears that we shed,
> As the night dew that falls on the grass o'er his head.
> But the night dew that falls, though in silence it weeps,
> Shall brighten with verdure the grave where he sleeps,
> And the tear that we shed, though in secret it rolls,
> Shall long keep his memory green in our souls.
>
> THOMAS MOORE

Aftermath

Robert Emmet was tried for treason and sentenced to be hanged, drawn and quartered. His small rebellion would hardly be remembered now if it were not for the speech that he made from the dock, at the end of his trial (see p.122). His words echoed for a hundred years, and were used to keep the torch of rebellion flickering even when hopes were lowest. His legend was also enhanced by Thomas Moore's romantic poem, 'Oh! breathe not his name'.

Robert Emmet was executed on 20 September 1803, aged twenty-five. His sweetheart was Sarah Curran, daughter of John Philpot Curran, a prominent barrister who had defended some of the

The attack on Lord Kilwarden, the most serious incident of Emmet's rising. Engraving by George Cruikshank. Mansell Collection, Katz Picture Library.

Robert Emmet speaking from the dock,
from a nineteenth-century woodcut.
Central Catholic Library.

men of 1798. She is said to have waved to him on his way to the scaffold. Handkerchiefs were dipped in his blood; a legend began to grow.

Although the outbreak had failed, it made the authorities very nervous, because it had been urban-based. They were used to dealing with rural unrest, but began now to worry about controlling the growing numbers of artisans in the developing towns.

I have had little time to look at the thousand difficulties which still lie between me and the completion of my wishes: that those difficulties will likewise disappear I have ardent, and, I trust, rational hopes; but if it is not to be the case, I thank God for having gifted me with a sanguine disposition. To that disposition I run from reflection; and if my hopes are without foundation — if a precipice is opening under my feet from which duty will not suffer me to run back, I am thankful for that sanguine disposition which leads me to the brink and throws me down, while my eyes are still raised to the visions of happiness that my fancy formed in the air.

ROBERT EMMET to Sarah Curran

Above: *Michael Dwyer's cottage where he hid from British army searches after the rebellion, until his surrender in December 1803. Courtesy Kenneth MacGowan.*

Left: *Thomas Russell — 'The Man from God-Knows-Where' in Florence Wilson's famous poem. Central Catholic Library.*

Anne Devlin

A sad footnote to the Emmet rebellion is provided by the story of
Anne Devlin, Robert Emmet's housekeeper. She was of a Wicklow family, and related to Michael Dwyer, the outlaw who had
established himself in the Wicklow Mountains. After the rising,
she carried messages between the hidden Emmet and his Dublin
contacts. When soldiers came to the house in Butterfield Lane,
Rathfarnham, looking for Emmet (known as 'Mr Ellis'), Anne
refused to give information and was half-hanged.

My father had sometime before sent over to Mr Emmet's residence
a light cart to help give the appearance of business. It was freshly
painted blue. This they put standing up, a rope was put over it and
about my neck ... I was hauled over and the rope was thrown
across the back band. They shouted again, 'Will you tell now
where Mr Ellis is?'

'No, villains, I will tell you nothing about him,' I said. I thought
of praying and had only time to say, 'Oh, Lord, have mercy on me'
when they gave a tremendous shout and pulled me up.

How long they kept me suspended I cannot say, but at last I felt
a kind of consciousness of my feet again touching the ground.
Their savage shouting had not ceased at this time, and I felt a hand
loosening the rope on my neck.

ANNE DEVLIN, *Jail Journal*

She and her family were arrested and brought to Kilmainham Jail
in Dublin. Here she still refused to speak, although she had a brief
encounter with Emmet in the prison yard when he urged her to
save herself, because she could not save him anyway. She was
offered £500 by Major Sirr, who had arrested Emmet, but she
rejected it. By Christmas of 1803 eight members of her family
were being held in jail, as well as ten members of Michael
Dwyer's family.

She said that after one year, 'if my spirits were still buoyant, close confinement, want of exercise, bad diet and other ill-usages were making gradual inroad on my constitution'. She was held in Kilmainham until 1806, and was released to a poverty-stricken and sickly existence. Her family had lost their farm, and one of her brothers had died in prison. She worked as a washerwoman, and was married for a time, having two children. A widow, she was befriended late in life by a Dr Madden who erected a monument over her grave in Glasnevin Cemetery. She died in 1851.

After my liberation, in the latter end of 1806, I frequently met with some of the former state prisoners in the streets; they passed on without seeming to recognise me. But something like an inward agitation was visible on their countenance. And although I may say I was then houseless and friendless, I never troubled a being of them, or anyone else with my distress, although I held the life's thread of more than fifty of the most respectable of them in my hands. But the pride of acting right consoled me, and I never took into account my incarceration, loss of health, the long and wasting confinement, and destruction of my whole family.

ANNE DEVLIN, *Jail Journal*

Reading The Nation *in a rural forge.*
Woodcut from Gavan Duffy, Young Ireland. *Central Catholic Library.*

3

THE REBELLION OF 1848

The thirty years or so after Robert Emmet's rebellion saw an ebb and flow of popular movements such as the agitation against tithes (compulsory payments to the Church of Ireland), and Daniel O'Connell's drive for Catholic Emancipation, which ended with a Catholic Relief Act in 1829. Politically, the Reform Act of 1832 allowed the election of an influential Irish grouping in the British Parliament, which was to be of increasing importance as the century wore on.

Economically, while towns began to develop industrially, the rural population remained caught in conditions of great poverty. They were utterly dependent on the potato crop, which was subject to periodic attacks of disease. Even times of economic prosperity (such as the Napoleonic Wars, which ended in 1815) made no difference to people who paid inflated rents to absentee landlords, through agents and middle-men who extorted every penny they could. Nevertheless, the population grew, and a census in 1841 indicated that Ireland supported eight million people, double the number at the start of the century.

The Young Irelanders

The year 1848 was a time of revolution in Europe, with outbreaks in Austria, Italy and France. In Britain, the Chartist movement,

The grim background to the Rising of 1848: carrying a dead victim of the Great Famine for burial. Contemporary lithograph by A. Maclure. National Library of Ireland.

seeking voting rights and social change, was making the authorities nervous. In Ireland, of course, the Great Famine had just reached its peak, and the population had been devastated by years of hunger and enforced emigration. Almost one and a half million people had died since 1845.

None the less, a group of young idealists devoted themselves to plans of revolution. These young men, known collectively as the 'Young Irelanders', had previously been supporters of Daniel O'Connell, the hero of Catholic Emancipation, and his mass movement for Repeal of the Act of Union. They had ultimately moved away from the ageing O'Connell, impatient with his insistence on using slow, constitutional methods to bring about change.

Clockwise from Top Left: *Thomas Davis, from a drawing by F.W. Burton; William Smith O'Brien; John Mitchel; Charles Gavan Duffy. All Central Catholic Library.*

One of the most influential Young Irelanders was Thomas Davis, a Protestant barrister from Cork, who developed a theory of Irish nationality. 'Surely,' he wrote, 'the desire of nationality is not ungenerous, nor is it strange in the Irish (looking to their history); nor, considering the population of Ireland, and the situation of their home, is the expectation of it very wild.' In mainland Europe, ideas of nationality were being developed in countries such as Italy and Germany, and Davis was determined to assert Ireland's right to a nationality of her own, despite the Act of Union.

Davis founded a radical newspaper, called *The Nation*, in 1842, with Charles Gavan Duffy, an Ulster Catholic, and John Blake Dillon, a Catholic lawyer. The paper advocated the development of a non-sectarian cultural nationalism; it called for Irish self-government and economic self-reliance:

> We must sink the distinctions of blood as well as sect. The Milesian, the Dane, the Norman, the Welshman, the Scotsman and the Saxon, naturalized here, must combine regardless of their blood — the Strongbownian must sit with the Ulster Scot and him whose ancestor came from Tyre or Spain must confide in and work with the Cromwellian and the Williamite....

The Nation was filled with articles on art and history, and reams of poetry extolling ancient days and glorious pasts. Its nationalism was essentially romantic. It did not actually advocate physical-force rebellion, although the language used was occasionally inflammatory. It reached over 100,000 people, an enormous circulation for the time, and was extremely useful to O'Connell's Repeal Movement for several years.

Breaking with O'Connell, the Young Irelanders were convinced that radical action was the only answer to Ireland's problems. In 1847, as the Great Famine decimated the population, they established the Irish Confederation. They started to set up local 'Confederate clubs' to spread their ideas of Irish nationality and self-reliance, but it was a slow process in the circumstances. By the end of 1847 only twenty-three of these clubs existed.

Simultaneously, a new tenant rights movement had begun to gather force. It was spearheaded by James Fintan Lalor, son of a strong farmer who had been part of the tithe resistance movement in the 1830s. Lalor rejected the idea of Repeal as irrelevant to Ireland's dire situation, and felt that the Confederation's idea of nationalism was too idealistic and impractical. To him, the only cause that Irish people would rally round was that of the land, and land ownership. He advocated 'moral insurrection', meaning the withholding of rents until the landlords could be brought to see reason. But this was as unreal as the ideas of the Young Irelanders; caught up in the daily struggle simply to survive, the starving peasantry could not be interested in political activity.

One of the protagonists of Lalor's movement was John Mitchel, a Unitarian with an eloquent pen, who had written for *The Nation*. He became increasingly irritated by the lack of practical planning, and broke away both from Lalor and from the Irish Confederation in early 1848. He founded a newspaper (provocatively called the *United Irishman*) in which he preached instant and violent revolution, and published articles on military tactics. The leaders of the Confederation distanced themselves from him, but he had a good deal of support among the ordinary members. The leaders were all from comfortable well-to-do backgrounds, and seemed to expect change to happen spontaneously. Certainly, they could see no future for violent action at this time.

Revolution in Europe

Meanwhile, revolutionary activity began to spread through Europe. The revolution in France was bloodless; the king had simply fled Paris under threat, and a citizens' government had taken over. This gave the Irish Confederation hope that a similar result could be achieved in Ireland. One of their members, Thomas Francis Meagher, visited Paris.

Son of a Waterford merchant, he was called 'Meagher of the

Sword' because of an impassioned speech he had made in 1846:

> I look upon the sword as a sacred weapon. And if ... it has sometimes reddened the shroud of the oppressor, like the anointed rod of the high priest, it has, at other times, blossomed into flowers to deck the free-man's brow.... Abhor the sword and stigmatise the sword? No, my lord....

Thomas Francis Meagher, from a contemporary woodcut.
Central Catholic Library.

Now he brought back from France a new flag for the Irish revolution — a green, white and orange tricolour, modelled on the French flag. The white, explained Meagher, signified a truce between 'Orange' and 'Green'.

Alarmed by the activity in Europe, and always nervous about the 'back door', the British government sent 10,000 troops into Ireland. The *United Irishman* was banned, but the *Irish Felon* immediately took its place. Mitchel, Meagher and William Smith O'Brien, Protestant MP for Limerick and founder member of the Irish Confederation, were arrested and tried for seditious speeches and writings. Two of the prosecutions failed, but when it came to Mitchel, who was feared as a powerful speaker, the authorities 'packed' the jury, and he was found guilty.

Sentenced to transportation, he was sent to Australia to spend fourteen years in hard labour. Although he had been widely regarded as an extremist, this severe treatment created a wave of publicity and public sympathy for his cause. (After some years in Tasmania, he escaped to the United States, where he spent the rest of his life.)

The Young Irelanders finally began to lay plans for a rebellion, collecting money and arms, although they must have realised that the people as a whole were in no condition to fight. There were seventy Confederate clubs altogether, almost half of them in Dublin. However, they were untrained and unarmed. Agents were sent to France and America for support, and renewed contact was made with the old Repeal Association, forming a new association, the Irish League.

Smith O'Brien and Gavan Duffy were still thinking only in terms of arming the Confederate clubs to make a display, in the hope of forcing government to grant their demands without actually having to fight. They were very unwilling to bring the issue of physical force to a head.

However, Meagher was suddenly arrested again under a new Treason Felony Act, along with Gavan Duffy, Thomas D'Arcy Magee (assistant editor of *The Nation*) and several others. All except Duffy were later released on bail.

Rebellion

Martial law was declared in several counties, and a bill suspending Habeas Corpus was rushed through parliament, usually a signal that wholesale arrests were to be made. Smith O'Brien, who had been travelling round the country to estimate its readiness for revolution, came back to Dublin, and was threatened with arrest himself. Matters had to be pushed to a conclusion, and some of the Young Ireland leaders began to move through the country, seeking support.

The only positive responses they got were in counties Kilkenny, Limerick and Tipperary. Otherwise, shattered by four years of insecurity, the people were apathetic, or nervous, or determined to wait until the harvest had been gathered in. Basically, as Kee puts it, O'Brien and the others were saying that they would take up arms if the people supported them, and the people were saying that they would support them if they took up arms.

'The Battle of Limerick', the London Punch*'s ribald view of the fracas in April 1848, when the Young Irelanders were routed by a combination of O'Connell's 'moral force' and the British authorities. Courtesy Peter Costello.*

Rural Ireland: market day in Thurles, August 1848.
M. Doheny, The Felon's Track.

A street in Ballingarry in 1848. Illustrated London News.

The McCormack house in Ballingarry before the Rising. The Felon's Track.

'The Battle of Widow McCormack's Cabbage Patch'.
Penny Illustrated Paper.

*The Royal Irish Constabulary barracks at Aheny Hill,
burnt out by the rebels.* The Felon's Track.

The only real conflict of the 'rebellion' took place in Tipperary, where William Smith O'Brien, with forty men carrying arms and about a hundred more armed with stones, took part in the so-called 'Battle of Ballingarry' on 29 July. Fired on by the police from a farmhouse ('Widow McCormack's cabbage-patch'), the rebels fled and the leaders went into hiding. Two rebels had been killed, and several police and rebels wounded. O'Brien later remarked bitterly, 'the people preferred to die of starvation at home, or to flee as voluntary exiles to other lands, rather than to fight for their lives and liberties', but it is difficult to imagine what else he could have expected.

Despite the temptation of reward money, none of the leaders was betrayed while in hiding. O'Brien was arrested trying to board a train, and other arrests were made over the following months. James Stephens, who had been active in Tipperary, escaped to

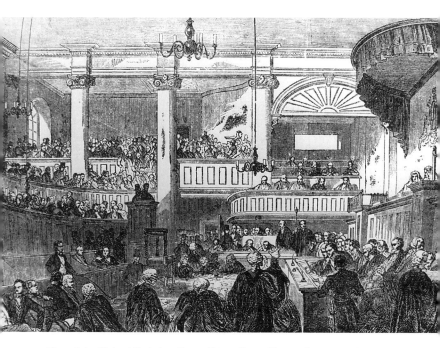

The trial of John Mitchel at Green Street Court House, the scene of many patriot trials. The Felon's Track.

France, as did Michael Doheny, a barrister who had worked with Lalor's tenant rights movement. Although some of the leaders were sentenced to death, none of these sentences was carried out.

O'Brien, Meagher, Terence Bellew McManus and John Martin (editor of the *Irish Felon*) were transported to Tasmania; McManus and Meagher eventually escaped to America. Smith O'Brien and Martin were pardoned in 1854, and allowed home. Thomas D'Arcy Magee ended up as postmaster-general of Canada, and Meagher became general of the Irish Brigade which fought with great bravery on the Union side during the American Civil War.

Aftermath

The results of the rebellion of 1848 were more far-reaching than its failure might have suggested. Those leaders who reached

America had been completely politicised by England's behaviour during the Irish famine, and kept this hatred of England fresh for the Irish emigrants in the United States and their descendants. In Paris, James Stephens and John O'Mahony maintained their anti-British fervour, and continued to plot. In Ireland, Charles Gavan Duffy revived *The Nation*, and helped to lay the foundations of the tenant rights movement of the 1850s. Most of the released leaders adopted a stance of non-violence, seeking change through constitutional means.

All of these influences played a large part in the development of the next stage in Ireland's movement towards independence, nationalism and self-determination. The Young Irelanders had been excellent publicists, and their eloquent writings and speeches remained in the public domain to do their work.

John Mitchel threw his energies into writing and journalism, and accused Britain of planned genocide through famine in his publication of 1861, *The Last History of Ireland (Perhaps)*. Returning to Ireland late in life, he was elected MP for Tipperary in 1875 on an anti-Home Rule platform, but died shortly afterwards.

In relation to the Great Famine, which had reached its worst depths in 1847–8, the abortive rebellion had a disastrous effect on the flow of charitable funds. The British people were already resentful of demands for aid which seemed to have no end, and now the ungrateful Irish were actually biting the hand that was trying, to some extent, to feed them. Lord John Russell, the prime minister, wrote:

> We have subscribed, worked, visited, clothed, for the Irish, millions of money, years of debate, etc., etc., etc. The only return is rebellion and calumny. Let us not grant, lend, clothe, etc., any more, and see what that will do ... British people think this.

The deported leaders: Kevin Izod O'Doherty **(top)**; *Thomas Francis Meagher* **(bottom left)***; and Terence Bellew McManus* **(bottom right)**.
The Felon's Track.

The Fenian ship, Erin's Hope, *carrying arms and men to the rising, saluting the green flag of the Irish Republic for the first time.*
A.M. Sullivan, Speeches from the Dock.

4

THE REBELLION OF 1867

The normal run of agrarian unrest and 'secret societies' continued at a low level of activity, and in 1858 the authorities became aware of yet another oath-taking body. One version of the oath ran as follows:

> I, ..., swear in the presence of God, to renounce all allegiance to the Queen of England, and to take arms and fight at a moment's warning, and to make Ireland an Independent Democratic Republic, and to yield implicit obedience to the commanders and superiors of this secret society....

The men arrested as members of this group, called 'The Phoenix National and Literary Society of Skibbereen', pleaded guilty, and were bound over to good behaviour.

This society and others had resulted from the undercover activities of one man, called 'An Seabhac' (The Hawk). This was in fact James Stephens, who had fled to France after the Young Ireland rebellion, and had never ceased to preach revolution. He had studied the organisation of various international secret societies, and was now travelling around Ireland spreading his revolutionary socialist and republican principles. He found it a dispiriting experience; all revolutionary fervour seemed to have died. He was convinced that it was important to have at least one outbreak of republican revolution in each generation, or the cause would be lost forever. However, it was clear that the land issue was far more important than nationalism to ordinary people.

Financial assistance was becoming available in America, as Irish emigrants improved their status and prospects. The 'Emmet Monument Association', founded in 1854, had already offered help for a rebellion. While Stephens knew that a lot of the Irish-American 'shamrockery' was merely emotional talk, he felt that more could be made of this chance. He redoubled his efforts, recruiting men such as Thomas Clarke Luby. Luby had been involved with Fintan Lalor in an abortive attempt at rebellion in 1849, consisting of an attack on a police barracks in Waterford.

In 1857, a message from America asked Stephens to set up a proper revolutionary organisation, with Irish-American support. Stephens founded the requested organisation on 17 March 1858; originally the Irish Revolutionary Brotherhood, it was to become known as the Irish Republican Brotherhood. He placed himself in sole command, and indeed his administration was extremely competent, although he was later accused of keeping too much authority in his own hands. In the early stages, Dublin Castle confused this group with various 'Phoenix' societies, so it was not properly identified for a long time. Its oath, drafted by Luby, called for the establishment of an independent democratic republic, and members promised 'to preserve inviolable secrecy'. It was the first completely secular secret society in Ireland, with no clerical support at all, and its leaders were of a lower social level than previous revolutionary leaders.

In order to speed up the transfer of funds, Stephens visited America in late 1858. He did not have much success in collecting money, but he did leave a new grouping behind him, headed by John O'Mahony. It was called the Fenian Brotherhood (after the ancient warrior-band of Irish legend, the Fianna). Stephens then moved to France, leaving Luby in Dublin as his Irish agent, and sent John O'Leary to America as his representative there. Stephens seemed to settle down to life in Paris, without advancing plans any further.

James Stephens, based on a contemporary photograph.
Central Catholic Library.

A financial crisis in America delayed the passage of money again, and for some years, little more happened. Then in 1861 Terence Bellew McManus died in poverty in San Francisco. McManus had been one of the Young Ireland rebels who had escaped from imprisonment in Tasmania, and the Fenian Brotherhood proposed that his body should be brought back to Ireland for burial. Brought in triumphant procession through New York, McManus's body lay in state in St Patrick's Cathedral until it left the country.

Stephens decided that this funeral could be used to ignite nationalist fervour, but constitutional nationalists, including the remaining Young Irelanders, were not in favour of this tactic. Neither was the Catholic Church, which condemned all secret societies; Paul Cullen, the Archbishop of Dublin, forbade a lying-in-state. However, a radical priest agreed to say the funeral prayers. McManus was buried in Glasnevin Cemetery, Dublin, on 10 November 1861, before a crowd estimated by the police at 8,000. The 20,000-strong procession to the cemetery was led by members of an IRB 'front', the National Brotherhood of St Patrick. The publicity was immense.

From this time the IRB began to be referred to as 'The Fenians', and Stephens toured the country seeking support for a rising. He founded a newspaper called the *Irish People*, which produced nationalist and republican propaganda. The organisation in America was disrupted by the American Civil War, but by 1864 Stephens was claiming that there were 100,000 members there.

In Ireland, John Devoy of the IRB concentrated on encouraging Irish soldiers in the British militia to take the Fenian oath. IRB groups were being drilled, and trained in the use of arms. Some people were arrested for illegal drilling, but by early 1865 Stephens was able to claim a membership of 85,000 in Ireland. The members were largely working-class young men from the towns; perhaps about a quarter were rural labourers. Most of the meetings took place in public houses, as there was nowhere else a group

THE BOLD FENIAN MEN

Oh see who comes over the red blossomed heather,
Their green banners kissing the pure mountain air,
Head erect, eyes in front, stepping proudly together,
Sure Freedom sits throned on each proud spirit there.
While down the hills twining, Their blessed steel shining,
Like rivers of beauty they flow from each glen;
From mountain and valley,
'Tis Liberty's rally —
Out and make way for the bold Fenian Men!

Our prayers and our tears have been scoffed and derided,
They've shut out God's sunlight from spirit and mind,
Our foes were united and we were divided,
We met, and they scattered us all to the wind.
But once more returning, Within our veins burning,
The fires that illumined dark Aherlow glen,
We raise the old cry anew,
Slogan of Con and Hugh —
Out and make way for the bold Fenian Men!

We've men from the Nore, from the Suir and the Shannon,
Let the tyrants come forth, we'll bring force against force —
Our pen is the sword and our voice is the cannon,
Rifle for rifle, and horse against horse.
We've made the false Saxon yield Many a red battlefield:
God on our side we will triumph again;
Pay them back woe for woe,
Give them back blow for blow —
Out and make way for the bold Fenian Men!

Side by side for the cause have our forefathers battled,
When our hills never echoed the tread of a slave
On many green hills where the leaden hail rattled,
Through the red gap of glory they march'd to their grave.
And those who inherit Their name and their spirit
Will march 'neath the banners of Liberty then
All who love Saxon law, Native or Sassenach,
Must out and make way for the bold Fenian Men!

MICHAEL SCANLAN (1836–?)

could meet without attracting suspicion, and drunkenness became a severe problem in maintaining secrecy and a tight organisation.

The IRB used an extremely secretive 'cell' system. While this protected groups from infiltration, it also meant intense suspicion of 'outsiders', and often led to delays in getting information through and plans carried out. Local groups were very independent of the centre, and would involve themselves in local agitations, ignoring Stephens' primary aim of secret revolutionary activity and planning.

Moves towards Rebellion

The authorities, which had had spies among the Fenians for some time, suddenly moved to arrest the leaders in late 1865. *The Irish People* was banned, and Luby, O'Leary and Jeremiah O'Donovan Rossa (from Cork) were arrested. Stephens remained free for a while, and sent word to the US that much of the Irish organisation was still in place, despite the arrests. He himself was finally arrested in November, along with Charles Kickham (later to become President of the Supreme Council of the IRB), and the secret 'military council' had to elect a temporary head. They chose an American officer, General Millen. Later arrests were made in February 1866, and included John Devoy.

Stephens escaped from prison with the help of two warders, who had sworn the Fenian oath. After some months in hiding in Dublin, he was smuggled to France. From there he hoped to reach America. He had already decided that any rebellion must be postponed, although one had been promised for 1865. Apart from the disruption caused by the arrests, word had reached him that the Fenians in the US had split.

The American Fenian split had been partly over money, and partly over ambition. The ranks of the American Fenians were now being strengthened by men with military experience, who had fought in the Civil War, which had ended in 1865. Many powerful personalities were contending for authority, and John O'Mahony, Stephens' choice of controller, was opposed by Colonel John Roberts. Roberts wanted to attack Canada (representing the British Empire) at the same time as a rising in Ireland would be taking place.

When Stephens arrived in the States, he did his best to strengthen the O'Mahony wing. Meanwhile, Roberts and his followers, about 3,000 men, crossed into Canada on 31 May 1866, and occupied a border village. On 2 June they won a minor battle, at Ridgeway, but found themselves disarmed by American forces. The American authorities had left the Fenians alone up to that point, but had no wish to start a war with Britain. The Fenians had no choice but to withdraw, having lost about seventy men, killed or captured.

Stephens was still talking about an imminent rising in Ireland, but 1866 was drawing on, and it seemed less and less likely. Yielding to practicalities, he tried to persuade the American Fenians that it would have to be postponed yet again. There were only 4,000 rifles in Ireland, he said. However, the American leadership accused him of cowardice. They deposed him as leader, and control passed to Colonel Thomas J. Kelly, another Civil War veteran.

The decision was taken to go to Ireland and start the rebellion themselves. They headed first for England, in January 1867. The party included John McCafferty, Ricard O'Sullivan Burke, William Halpin, Gordon Massey, Michael O'Brien of Cork, and two Frenchmen named Gustave Cluseret and Octave Fariola — all experienced soldiers. Arriving in London, they laid plans for a rising in February.

The actual rising would take place in Ireland, but first weapons had to be provided. The plan was to seize arms and ammunition from an English military garrison at Chester Castle. Then all the trains would be commandeered by force, and the arms would be rushed to the Holyhead mailboat for Ireland.

Captain Massey set off for Ireland first, to begin preparations there. Later, he was found to have given evidence to the authorities, but it is not certain from what date he started to do this.

Rebellion

Early on the appointed day, 11 February, over a thousand men began to arrive in Chester. Suddenly, McCafferty was informed that the authorities were aware of the plan. With immense effort he succeeded in calling off the operation, and in postponing the outbreak in Ireland, but he could not prevent large numbers of Fenians from being arrested. They had been betrayed by John Corydon, a Fenian who had been passing information to the authorities for some time.

In Ireland, there were apparently 14,000 men ready in Dublin and 20,000 in Cork, but shortage of weapons was the main problem. Massey concluded that a rising would have no hope of success, but the other leaders insisted on going ahead, even after the arrests in England. They picked a new date, 5 March, but again they were betrayed by Corydon, who had not yet been unmasked. Some of the leaders were arrested, but news of this was too late to reach all the areas involved, and small uprisings took place in Dublin, Drogheda, Cork, Tipperary, Clare and Limerick.

The Irish police force reacted with strength and discipline, and small groups of police were able to disperse large forces of the rebels. For example, at Tallaght, Co. Dublin ('the Battle of Tallaght'), fourteen police succeeded in dispersing several hundred rebels. The police force was later granted the appellation 'Royal' for its activities during this crisis. As news spread of the leaders' arrests, other groups of rebels began to disperse, hoping to get home without being noticed.

There were small successes in Co. Cork, but without overall leadership the rebels could go no further. A skirmish took place at

Ballyhurst, near Tipperary, but the rebels fled when soldiers returned fire. The main aim of the rebellion had been, after the initial assaults, to maintain a level of guerrilla warfare, but the capture of the leaders meant that this plan disintegrated.

In April — already too late — a ship set sail from New York with Fenian officers, rifles, cannon and ammunition, under Generals Nagle and Millen. The ship, rechristened *Erin's Hope*, was met at Sligo Bay by Ricard O'Sullivan Burke. He informed the generals that there was no hope of any response from the people in Sligo, so they sailed on, looking for somewhere to land. They got as far as Waterford before provisions began to run out, and they decided to land some of the officers and return to New York.

Twenty-eight officers were landed, and all were arrested almost immediately. The police escorting them were attacked by a mob, and Corydon was stoned when he came to give evidence at their trials. The Fenians evidently had a lot of popular support and sympathy, but the people would not come out and fight with them. Their proclamation had called for a rising of the labouring classes against the aristocracy, Irish or English, throughout the British Isles, while also seeking an Irish Republic.

View of the Knockmealdown Mountains, into which the Fenians fled, seen from Ardfinan. Illustrated London News.

The Battle of Tallaght, with Inspector Burke of the Constabulary directing his men to fire on the Fenians.
Penny Illustrated Paper.

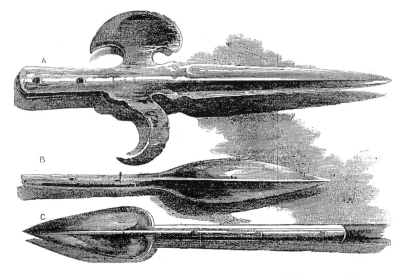

Above: *Contrasting pike-heads: A) pike-head of 1848, captured from John Mitchel; B & C) Fenian pike-heads displayed by the police in Dublin Castle*. Penny Illustrated Paper.

Below: *Fenian prisoners in Mountjoy Prison, Dublin, after the Battle of Tallaght*. Illustrated London News.

Capt. William Mackey Lomasney, the American-born Fenian leader who created the original 'flying column' in Cork in 1867: 'Had Fenians everywhere followed the example set by Captain Mackey in Cork they might have discovered the virtues of guerrilla tactics which brought victory to the IRA fifty years later' (Kilmainham Museum). He was blown to bits while trying to mine Westminster Bridge in London in 1883. From a contemporary photograph. Courtesy H. Litton.

Manchester Martyrs

As in the case of the Emmet rebellion, the real effectiveness of the Fenian rising lay in its aftermath. The headquarters in England remained active, but in September Colonel T.J. Kelly, who had been elected chief executive of the Irish Republic, was arrested in Manchester. With him was Captain Timothy Deasy. As they were being brought to prison, on 18 September, the van was stopped by thirty armed Fenians. The police sergeant inside, called Brett, refused to surrender, and Peter Rice fired a shot through the ventilator, killing him. The keys were seized and the prisoners escaped.

Kelly and Deasy were not recaptured, but large numbers of Irish in Manchester were arrested for questioning. It is clear that much of the police procedure was doubtful, and the evidence they used was questionable. Of the five men eventually charged with

Sergeant Brett's murder, only four had actually been present at the events. Rice had escaped to the US, with Kelly and Deasy, and a man called William Allen was charged with having fired the fatal shot.

The others charged with him were a man called Maguire (merely a marine on leave who hadn't been involved at all), and three Fenians, Edward Condon, Philip Larkin and Michael O'Brien. All were found guilty of murder. The convicted Fenians all made speeches from the dock, proclaiming their republican principles, but expressing regret for the murder. Condon ended: 'You will soon send us before God, and I am perfectly prepared to go. I have nothing to regret, or to retract or take back. I shall only say, "God Save Ireland"!' This was echoed by them all, and became a catch-cry for Irish nationalism.

Manchester Martyrs: the attack on the police van.
Illustrated London News.

Manchester Martyrs crying out 'God Save Ireland'.
Speeches from the Dock.

Knowing nothing of the locality I rushed up what appeared to be a street, but proved to be only a blind alley with no outlet. When I started back to make my way out the crowd gave way, but a detective struck me on the head with a heavy club, and this brought me to my knees for an instant. Rising, however, again I pushed on, tearing myself loose from those who tried to grab me, until I came to a narrow bridge crossing a canal. Here, among others, there were planted in my path two big, half-drunken women, who flung themselves on me, locking their arms around my neck, as if I were their long-lost brother. I had never tackled a proposition of that kind before, and no time was allowed me to consider how to deal with it. The detectives and mob closed in, and, after being badly battered on the head, I was seized and overpowered.

EDWARD CONDON

The authorities recognised in time that Maguire had had nothing to do with the affair, and he was pardoned. But the evidence used in his conviction had been much the same as that used against the others. His pardon cast doubt on all the convictions, and public disquiet grew, especially in Ireland. Condon, as an American citizen, was reprieved, but Allen, Larkin and O'Brien were hanged on 24 November 1867, the first Irishmen since Robert Emmet to be executed for political action.

Irish public opinion decided that they had been executed on false evidence, and simply for being Irish republicans. They were regarded as martyrs, and massive protest demonstrations were held. Up to then, the authorities had managed the Fenian threat successfully. The sentences after the actual rebellion had been relatively lenient. O'Donovan Rossa had been sentenced to life imprisonment,

---

GOD SAVE IRELAND

High upon the gallows tree swung the noble-hearted three,
    By the vengeful tyrant stricken in their bloom;
But they met him face to face, with the courage of their race,
    And they went with soul undaunted to their doom.

CHORUS
'God save Ireland,' said the heroes;
    'God save Ireland,' said they all.
'Whether on the scaffold high or on battlefield we die,
    O what matter when for Erin dear we fall.'

Girt around with cruel foes, still their courage proudly rose,
    For they thought of hearts that loved them far and near;
Of the millions true and brave o'er the ocean's swelling wave,
    And the friends in holy Ireland ever dear.

Climbed they up the rugged stair, rang their voices out in prayer,
    Then with England's fatal cord around them cast,
Close beside the gallows tree, they kissed like brothers lovingly,
    True to home and faith and freedom to the last.

Never till the latest day shall the memory pass away
    Of the gallant lives thus given for our land;
But on the cause must go, amid joy or weal or woe,
    Till we make our isle a nation free and grand.

                          T.D. SULLIVAN (1827–1914)

the heaviest sentence given, but he was released after six years. All death sentences had been commuted to imprisonment. The affair of the 'Manchester Martyrs' was clumsily handled in comparison.

Aftermath

The Fenians were involved in one more incident before this latest outburst of republican feeling died down. Ricard O'Sullivan Burke had been sent to Clerkenwell prison, on remand, and an attempt to rescue him by blowing down the prison wall went wrong. The authorities had been warned by unusual activity around the prison, and had changed the exercise routine. The explosion which took place killed twelve bystanders and injured thirty more, some seriously.

British public opinion awoke to the fact that the IRB was dangerous, and fear of further activity spread. In London alone, more than 5,000 special constables were sworn in. Concern was expressed that the 'Irish problem' should be solved, to prevent such activity from continuing, and this new public interest helped W.E. Gladstone, the Liberal Party leader, in his attempts to introduce Home Rule throughout the rest of the century.

In the preceding winter I underwent some forty days' punishment inside of three months. It had been an exceptionally cold winter, and, after taking from me portions of my clothing, I was put into the coldest cell in the prison — one that was known as the Arctic cell. Some time before I had to complain to the director about this cell being so frightfully cold that I had known the thermometer on frosty days, with a north-eastern blowing, to stand some degrees below freezing point. I got forty days' starvation and solitary confinement in that cell. Talk of hunger and cold! Many a time I was forced to chew the rags I got to clean my tinware in an effort to allay the hunger pangs.

TOM CLARKE, *An Irish Felon's Prison Life*

Political conditions began to improve in Ireland. The Church of Ireland was disestablished in 1869, and various Land Acts did a great deal to help tenants and labourers. Republican emotions were channelled into an Amnesty campaign, begun in 1869 by John 'Amnesty' Nolan, which fought for the release of all Fenian prisoners. Those who had been sentenced to penal

The memorial in Glasnevin to John Keegan Casey, the Fenian poet 'Leo'. His songs, notably 'The Rising of the Moon', kept the patriot spirit of the Fenians alive to 1916. Photo Walter Benton; courtesy Peter Costello.

Fenian Amnesty meeting in Phoenix Park, 1871.
Illustrated London News.

servitude were experiencing a harsh and often brutal régime, and the amnesty campaign helped to establish a government enquiry into prison conditions. O'Donovan Rossa was put forward as an election candidate, and he won a by-election in Tipperary in 1870, although as a prisoner he could not be allowed to enter parliament.

In 1870 Isaac Butt MP, once president of the Amnesty Association, established the Home Government Association, by 1873 called the Home Rule League. Its aim was to work (democratically) for an Irish parliament with responsibility for its own affairs. Although not looking for an independent republic, it was supported by many IRB members. The IRB became bitterly divided over this tactic, and MPs who supported Butt were later expelled from the society.

John O'Leary **(top)**, *Charles J. Kickham* **(bottom left)**, *and Thomas Clarke Luby* **(bottom right)** — *Fenian leaders whose influence lasted into another generation.* Speeches from the Dock.

Eviction scenes during the
Land War of 1880, in which
the Hillside Men were active,
creating a link between
rebellion and the parliamen-
tary Irish party.
Above: *Battered cottage.*
Lawrence Collection,
National Library
Right: *Evicted girl.*
Illustrated London News.

Brutalising searches were a feature of the aftermath of all the Irish rebellions. Here RIC men search a cottage for Fenian arms during the Land War. Central Catholic Library.

The Home Rule League became the road to political influence for Charles Stewart Parnell MP, who also became president of Michael Davitt's Land League, a movement fighting for tenant rights. In 1882 Parnell founded the National League, to push further for Home Rule. He gained the confidence of Gladstone, who was enthusiastically pressing the cause of Irish parliamentary independence. However, when Parnell was named in a divorce action by Captain Willie O'Shea in 1889, the scandal destroyed his career.

The fight for Home Rule passed into the hands of John Redmond, who became leader of the Irish MPs in Westminster in 1900. (Gladstone had died in 1898; his two Home Rule bills had been defeated.) Physical force rebellion seemed a thing of the past, supported by only a few die-hard Fenians. Constitutional activity was being promoted as the best way forward.

But in 1898 the centenary of the United Irishmen's rising was celebrated widely and enthusiastically. The real meaning of the movement was smothered under an emotional depiction of a purely Gaelic and Catholic uprising, led by noble and self-sacrificing priests. The ideal of a non-sectarian, all-embracing liberal democracy was swept aside.

Patrick Henry Pearse, the leading figure of the Easter Rising, and part-author of the 1916 Proclamation.
Collected Works of Patrick H. Pearse. *Central Catholic Library.*

5

THE REBELLION OF 1916

By the outbreak of the First World War, the situation in Ireland had become dangerously unstable. The fight for Home Rule, which had dominated Irish and British politics for so long, had finally resulted in a Home Rule Act, signed into law in 1914. It had been agreed, reluctantly, by the Irish Parliamentary Party that Ulster counties could opt out of Home Rule for six years, before coming under a Dublin parliament. But Ulster Unionists, appalled at the idea of living in an Irish state dominated by Catholics, and determined not to break the link with Britain, were making aggressive threats of instant secession. The Home Rule Act was suspended for the duration of the war; Ireland would have to wait.

This political ferment coincided with a cultural movement known as the Gaelic Literary Revival. Irish culture, literature, music and language were attracting increased attention, and people all over the country were learning about this newly discovered distinguished past. A vivid sense of nationalism was being established. Prominent among the Irish groups springing up were the Gaelic League and the Gaelic Athletic Association (GAA).

In 1899 Arthur Griffith, a journalist who had been a member of the IRB, established a paper called the *United Irishman*. He was no advocate of physical force rebellion; he wanted Ireland to separate peacefully from Britain and rely on her own resources, behind protective tariff barriers. Cumann na nGaedheal, a cultural organisation, was founded to promote these ideas, and to resist Anglicisation. Meanwhile in Ulster two IRB members, Bulmer Hobson and Denis McCullough, began founding 'Dungannon Clubs', from 1905. These also had a separatist agenda, and in 1907 they came together with Cumann na nGaedheal to form Sinn Féin ('Ourselves Alone').

In 1903, the centenary of Robert Emmet's rebellion was commemorated by huge parades and demonstrations. The *Freeman's Journal* said that this centenary should encourage Irish people to 'resolve one and all to do everything possible to hasten the day when his epitaph can be written'. John O'Leary, who headed the Centenary Committee, gave a short speech on the same theme, ending, 'I have nothing more to say, but I and all of you have very much to do'.

In the north, an Ulster Volunteer Force was established in January 1913 after a massive number of Unionists had signed a Solemn League and Covenant, which pledged them to resist Home Rule. Some of them signed in blood. The Ulster Volunteers, 100,000 strong, were to defend Ulster from any attempt to impose Home Rule. Arms were imported and distributed.

In retaliation for this move, and with anger that the British had made no effort to disarm the obviously illegal Ulster force, a huge public meeting was held in Dublin in November 1913, and the Irish Volunteers were born. Within six months, they numbered 75,000. Arms were imported for them, and attempts to confiscate these weapons led to the killing of three people by British soldiers in Bachelor's Walk, Dublin, in mid-1914.

IRB Infiltration

The IRB had remained relatively dormant during the period of the Home Rule movement. Some IRB members in fact supported these constitutional moves; Parnell was backed by John O'Leary,

James Stephens and John Devoy. But the organisation as a whole never lost sight of what it saw as essential, a physical rebellion. Home Rule was second best, and they were convinced that nothing more could be won from Britain without blood being spilled. A split with the American Fenians had been healed in 1876, and a new constitution had been developed.

This constitution enshrined three democratic principles:

1. The IRB, while preparing for war, was to confine itself to 'moral influence' in time of peace;

2. The IRB could not resort to war until the time for so doing had been decided by a majority of the Irish nation;

3. The IRB was to support every movement which could advance the cause of Irish independence, consistent with the maintenance of its own integrity.

With this in view, IRB members involved themselves in any organisation which could be used as a 'front' for rebellious activity. They inserted themselves in the Gaelic League, the GAA, Sinn Féin and, of course, the Irish Volunteers. They operated on a highly secretive level; few politicians believed that the IRB still existed. Its membership was to remain passive until it was called into action, and it recruited very carefully.

Chief among the activists was Thomas Clarke, a Fenian who had spent fifteen years in solitary confinement in Britain. He had been convicted of dynamiting offences during an unsuccessful campaign of terror in England in the 1880s. This had been organised from America by Clan na Gael, the US branch of the IRB, run by John Devoy. Released in 1898, Clarke had rejoined an old IRB fellow-prisoner, John Daly of Limerick, married Daly's niece, Kathleen, and gone back to the United States.

Returning to Ireland in 1907 with his family, he began to build up a network of contacts, with a view to bringing about a physical-force rebellion. His group of adherents included Hobson, McCullough and Seán MacDermott, a full-time organiser for Sinn Féin.

*Soup Kitchen in Liberty Hall during the Lock-Out of 1913. Drawing
by Sir William Orpen. W. Orpen,* Stories of Old Ireland and Myself.

Another element in the volatile political mix was provided by
the growing labour and trade union movement, which in 1913 had
suffered a devastating setback with the defeat of a general strike
in Dublin, after months of hardship. James Connolly, founder of
the Irish Labour Party, decided to set up a citizens' army to
protect workers in the future. The Irish Citizen Army was
founded in 1914, and was at first organised by the playwright
Seán O'Casey.

Above: The Irish Volunteers in College Green. Detail of a painting by Francis Wheatley. This body, raised to assert Irish legislative independence in 1782, was the origin of the name adopted by the new patriotic movement in 1914. *National Gallery of Ireland.*

Below: The Irish House of Commons, abolished with the union of Ireland and Britain which later Irish rebels fought to break. Painting by Francis Wheatley. *Lotherton Hall Collection, Leeds City Art Galleries/ Bridgeman Art Library.*

Above: Bagenal Harvey of Bargy Castle, leading the rebels at the battle
of New Ross. Watercolour attributed to John Boyne. *Crawford
Municipal Art Gallery Cork*. **Below**: The Battle of Oulart Hill (27 May
1798). Painting by Edward Foran OSA. *Courtesy of the Augustinian
Priory, New Ross. Photo: P.J. Browne*.

Above: Battle of New Ross. Painting by Edward Foran OSA. *Courtesy of the Augustinian Priory, New Ross. Photo: P.J. Browne.*

Right: Miniature of Robert Emmet by John Comerford. *Courtesy of the National Gallery of Ireland.*

THE IRISH PEOPLE'S EDITION.

YOUNG

PRICE 2/-

IRELAND

PART 2.

FOUR YEARS of IRISH HISTORY

Sir Charles Gavan Duffy

BY

M. H. GILL AND SON, DUBLIN

Young Ireland in arms: the leaders of 1848, from the cover of an 1880s popular edition of Gavan Duffy's history of the movement, a book which kept alive the separatist tradition. *Central Catholic Library.*

Above: The flag of the Irish Republic captured after the Easter Rising in 1916 by the British Army. *Courtesy of Michael Kenny, National Museum of Ireland*. **Below**: The Plough and the Stars, the flag of the socialist Irish Citizen Army, whose roots also went back to the 1840s. *Central Catholic Library*.

Above: The surrender of the College of Surgeons garrison, led by the Countess Markievicz. Painting by K. King. *Courtesy Yeats Museum, Sligo. Photo: David Davison.*

Left: 'The Volunteer', an idealised portrait of a 1916 veteran by nationalist painter Patrick Tuohy, whose father was Medical Officer in the GPO during Easter Week. *Private collection.*

Above: 'The Bread Line, 1916' — based on actual scenes at the time. Painting by Muriel Brandt RHA. *Crawford Art Gallery, Cork.*
Below: 'Study for the Court of Criminal Appeal' by Sir John Lavery. Roger Casement's appeal was heard in the Court of Appeal in London. *Hugh Lane Municipal Gallery of Modern Art.*

Above: Wolfe Tone's grave at Bodenstown, Co. Kildare, a place of modern Republican pilgrimage. *Courtesy National Graves Association.*

Below: Arbour Hill, Dublin, where the 1916 leaders are buried; general view, with stone screen on which is carved the text of the Proclamation. *Photo: Peter Costello.*

REASONS WHY

YOU SHOULD JOIN

The Irish Citizen Army.

BECAUSE It pledges its members to work for, organise for, drill for and fight for **an Independent Ireland.**

BECAUSE It places its reliance upon the only class that never betrayed Ireland—the Irish Working Class.

BECAUSE Having a definite aim to work for there is no fear of it being paralysed in the moment of action by divisions in its Executive Body.

BECAUSE It teaches that "the sole right of ownership of Ireland is vested in the people of Ireland, and that that full right of ownership may, and ought to be, enforced by any and all means that God hath put within the power of man."

BECAUSE It works in harmony with the Labour and true National Movements and thus embraces all that makes for Social Welfare and National Dignity.

Companies Wanted in Every District.

RECRUITS WANTED EVERY HOUR.

Apply for further information, Secretary, Citizen Army, Liberty Hall, Dublin.

Irish Paper.]   *City Printing Works, 13 Stafford Street, Dublin.*

Recruiting poster for the Irish Citizen Army, formed after the Lock-Out to defend the interest of the Irish working class.
Central Catholic Library.

*Members of the Irish Citizen Army, on guard on the roof of Liberty Hall,
headquarters of James Connolly. Central Catholic Library.*

Preparations for a Rising

This complicated tapestry forms the background to the Easter
Rising of 1916. The IRB had seized on the outbreak of the First
World War as an unparalleled opportunity to take advantage of
British involvement on the continent, and made contact with
Germany in the hope of receiving weapons and financial support.
Sir Roger Casement, who had served in the British consular
service in Africa, became the IRB's agent in this. They were
already receiving some Irish-American assistance from Clan na
Gael in the United States.

John Redmond, leader of the Irish Parliamentary Party, called
for the Irish Volunteers to join the British army, to defend small
nations against the ambitions of Germany. The Volunteers split

on the issue, and Redmond was supported by 170,000 men, who now called themselves the National Volunteers. The remainder (a minority of about 12,000) kept the original name.

However, they did not remain a minority for long. When war broke out, over 50,000 Irishmen had enlisted in the British army. Many others immediately began to emigrate to the United States, probably fearing later conscription, and the British responded by tightening passport regulations and limiting shipping lists. This meant that large numbers of young men, mostly unemployed, were trapped within Ireland, with few outlets for their energies. The Volunteers provided them with something to do.

The IRB intensified its plans for insurrection. Eoin MacNeill, a professor from University College Dublin, was chief of staff of the Irish Volunteers, aided by Bulmer Hobson and The

The Countess Markievicz, a leading figure in the Rising. Courtesy Peter Costello.

O'Rahilly. Although Hobson and The O'Rahilly were IRB members, they were not planning violent revolution. Those who were, however, also held influential positions in the Volunteers. These were Patrick Pearse, director of military organisation; Joseph Plunkett, director of military operations; and Thomas Mac-Donagh, director of training. The IRB had a controlling majority on the Volunteer General Council. MacNeill was completely unaware of any of this.

In May 1915, a military council of the IRB was set up to control planning, with Tom Clarke, Pearse, Plunkett, Eamonn Ceannt and Thomas MacDonagh. At a later stage James Connolly was included, because he had been threatening to lead his Citizen Army in rebellion if no one else moved. This military council agreed on Easter 1916 as the date for a rising. Surprise was essential, so any planning was kept extremely secret; very little information got through. This tight control ultimately meant that when things went wrong, great confusion resulted.

And the change that has come over the young men of the country who are volunteering! Erect, heads up in the air, the glint in the eye, and then the talent and ability that had been latent and is now being discovered! Young fellows who had been regarded as something like wastrels now changed to energetic soldiers and absorbed in the work, and taking pride that at last they feel they can do something for their country that will count. 'Tis good to be alive in Ireland these times.

TOM CLARKE to John Devoy, 14.5.1914

In June 1915 Jeremiah O'Donovan Rossa, one of the first generation of Fenians, died in the United States, and his body was brought back to Ireland for burial. The IRB made full use of this funeral for propaganda purposes, and a massive procession to Glasnevin Cemetery, Dublin, on 1 August was crowned by a

Poster for the Irish Volunteers, 1914. Courtesy Peter Costello.

stirring oration from Patrick Pearse. He declaimed: 'The defenders of this realm think they have pacified Ireland ... but the fools, the fools, the fools! They have left us our Fenian dead, and while Ireland holds these graves, Ireland unfree can never be at peace.'

MacNeill began to get suspicious. To him there could be no justification for a physical-force rebellion without extreme provocation, and only then with a very strong probability of success, and he felt that neither of these conditions existed at that time. When he was finally informed that a rising was planned for 24

April 1916 — Easter Sunday — he was appalled, and immediately published a notice in the *Sunday Independent* cancelling the 'manoeuvres' planned for that day.

This caused great confusion in Volunteer ranks up and down the country. Devastated at the prospect of missing the opportunity for which they had worked for so long, Clarke and the others sent messengers in all directions, altering the date to Easter Monday. But of course these messages did not reach everyone, or were not always believed. Many local commanders, confused and uncertain, decided to sit tight.

Meanwhile, Roger Casement had suffered disaster in his attempts to land in Kerry, accompanying a shipment of German arms. The ship that carried them was scuttled by her captain, after a muddle of missed dates, and Casement and two companions were arrested. When word of this reached Dublin, the conspirators realised without question that the rising had no hope of success. They would be hopelessly short of weapons, and Casement's arrest would have alerted the authorities that something was up. Nevertheless, they decided to go on with their plans, and make a mark on their own generation at least.

Easter Rising

The plans for the rising were well-laid and organised, and it might have had some chance of success if all the Volunteers had come out as arranged, if enough weapons had been available, and if the British had responded as they were expected to. However, the commandants who assembled on Easter Monday morning found that most of their troops had simply not turned up, and those who had were poorly armed and very short of ammunition. Moreover, James Connolly's assertion that the British would not bomb or shell Dublin's economic and financial centre proved lamentably wide of the mark.

EQUITMENT.

ꜰⁱⱥⁿⁿⱥ ꜰⱥⁱꞁ.
THE IRISH VOLUNTEERS

SERVICE KIT.

The following are the articles prescribed by Headquarters for the personal equipment of Volunteers on field service. Items printed in **heavy type** are to be regarded as important:

FOR ALL VOLUNTEERS.

(a.) As to clothes: uniform or other clothes as preferred; if uniform not worn clothes to be of neutral colour; nothing white or shiny (white collar not to be worn); **soft-brimmed hat** (to be worn in lieu of cap on field service); strong comfortable boots; overcoat.

(b.) As to arms: **rifle,** with sling and **cleaning outfit;** 100 rounds of **ammunition,** with **bandolier** or **ammunition pouches** to hold same; **bayonet,** with scabbard, frog and belt; strong knife or slasher.

(c.) As to provision for rations: **haversack, water-bottle,** mess-tin (or billy can) with knife, fork, spoon, tin cup; 1 dry stick (towards making fire); emergency ration.

(d.) **Knapsack** containing: spare shirt, pair of socks, towel, soap, comb; scissors, needle, thread, safety-pins.

(e.) In the pocket: clasp-knife, note-book and pencil, matches in tin box, boot laces, strong cord, a candle, **coloured** handkerchiefs.

(f.) Sewn inside coat: **First Field Dressing.**

FOR OFFICERS.

(a.) As to clothes: uniform is very desirable for officers; if not worn sufficient but not unduly conspicuous distinguishing mar¹ f rank to be worn.

(b.) ⸱ ⸱ arms: **automatic pistol** or **revolver,** with **ammunition** for sa e, in lieu of rifle; sword, sword bayonet, or short lance.

The rest f the equipment as for ordinary Volunteers, with the following

(c.) Additions: **Whistle** on cord; **Watch; Field Despatch-book;** Fountain Pen or **Copying-ink Pencil;** Field-Glasses; Pocket Compass; Range Finder; **Map** of District; electric torch, hooded.

Sub-Officers and **Scouts** should as far as possible be provided with the additional articles prescribed for Officers

By Order

The Equipment Order ⸱⸱⸱ the Irish Volunteers

How the rebels were equipped: list of items carried in the Irish Volunteers' service kit. Courtesy Peter Costello.

However, the plotters were helped by government incompetence. Right up to the Rising, sources in Dublin Castle were saying that there was no evidence of treasonable activity in the country; they believed that there were only a thousand or so IRB men, and that the organisation was moribund. Secret service intelligence had not been functioning effectively for some time, and warning signs were ignored. On the actual day of the Rising, large numbers of British officers and troops were out of the city, enjoying the Bank Holiday races, and many key buildings were very lightly defended.

A body of men under Pearse and Connolly took over the General Post Office in O'Connell Street (then Sackville Street), and a stirring proclamation was read to the bemused populace. Other commandants placed themselves in strategic positions, prepared to defend the city centre from approach in any direction.

Are the women of Ireland as ready and willing to do their duty to their country as their Volunteer brothers? . . .

We can form ambulance corps, learn first aid, make all the flags to be carried by the Volunteers, do all the embroidery that may be required, such as badges on uniforms, etc. Classes for women in first aid should be organised at once in every town where a corps of Volunteers has been formed. Trained nurses will be found almost everywhere whose services could be acquired to give lessons. Apart from the services we can render to the Volunteers, first aid should form part of every girl's training. Almost every town has its technical classes and girls have good opportunities of learning designing, drawing, etc. They will have a chance of putting their knowledge to practical use now in the making of flags for the Volunteers. To a patriotic Irishwoman could there be any work of more intense delight than that?

CÁITLÍN de BRÚN, *Irish Volunteer*, 4 April 1914

Pearse, Connolly, Clarke, MacDonagh, Ceannt, Plunkett and MacDermott declared themselves to be a provisional government, at the head of a republic. However, there were at most about 1,000 rebels (118 of these belonging to the Citizen Army), with at least three times this number of British soldiers and police ranged against them, not to mention the troops who were poured into the city during the following week.

As we came abreast the main entrance of the GPO, in the middle of O'Connell Street, the command rang out: 'Company halt. Left turn.' Knowing what was coming next Collins and I anticipated events a little by linking our arms in Plunkett's and moving off towards the doorway. Then Connolly's stentorian voice rang out: 'The GPO, charge!' It was well we had anticipated the movement even by seconds as otherwise Plunkett might have been swept off his feet as the party with one wild cheer made a determined rush for the doorway. The large public office was crowded with people and officials. Just as we got inside Connolly's voice again rang out in a very determined tone, 'Everyone outside.'

For a moment there was a stunned silence. It seemed for that fraction of time as if the people and officials were under the impression that the peremptory order had reference only to the members of the Citizen Army. As soon as it was realised that it referred only to the public and officials present there was a panic rush for the exits. Several officials left their counters and bolted without waiting to secure either hats or coats. The moment the public offices were closed Connolly's voice again rang out: 'Smash the windows and barricade them!'

This order was carried out with great gusto. A female voice outside rose piercingly above the din, 'Glory be to God, the divils are smashing all the lovely windows.'

W.J. BRENNAN-WHITMORE,
Dublin Burning: The Easter Rising from Behind the Barricades

About ten o'clock we suddenly noticed a well-dressed, middle-aged man coming up to O'Connell Bridge from the direction of Butt Bridge. The light of the electric arc lamps shines on his carefully-brushed tall hat. Both sides shout to him to get away. He seems dazed, and walks about uncertainly for a few minutes. Suddenly a volley rings out from D'Olier Street, and he jumps about four feet into the air. Then with another bound he reaches the corner of the bridge and rushes down Eden Quay at racing pace. There seems something unreal about the thing. Seen in the unnatural light from the street standards, one cannot imagine it to be real live drama. Involuntarily one thinks of a cinematograph show. Suddenly an officer enters the room. He orders three or four crack shots to smash the arc lamps. A few seconds later O'Connell Street is plunged in darkness. Only the stars shed a mystic glare over the house-tops.

Extracts from notes by an Irish Volunteer
The Belvederian, 1917

The rebel leaders were surprised at the first civilian response to this breakdown of normal life, which expressed itself in looting the city-centre shops. They were verbally attacked by local women who were married to British soldiers fighting abroad, and could not receive the 'separation allowance' while the city's administration ground to a halt.

The Rising lasted for six days before the leaders surrendered, to save further loss of life. They had apparently not expected that there would be civilian casualties, but it is not possible to clear a capital city of its inhabitants overnight. Some of the civilian losses were the result of British soldiers shooting people in houses near the GPO, as they searched for rebels. Others, including the noted pacifist Francis Sheehy Skeffington, were executed by a British officer who was later declared insane. The full number of casualties was finally estimated at 64 rebels killed, 132 British troops and police, and 300 civilians. About 2,000 civilians were wounded.

Right: *The Tricol-
our flying over the
GPO during Easter
Week. Central
Catholic Library.*

Below: *Proclama-
tion of Martial Law
by the Viceroy,
dated 26 May 1916.
Central Catholic
Library.*

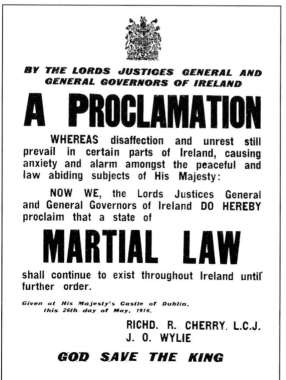

BY THE LORDS JUSTICES GENERAL AND
GENERAL GOVERNORS OF IRELAND

A PROCLAMATION

WHEREAS disaffection and unrest still
prevail in certain parts of Ireland, causing
anxiety and alarm amongst the peaceful and
law abiding subjects of His Majesty:

NOW WE, the Lords Justices General
and General Governors of Ireland DO HEREBY
proclaim that a state of

MARTIAL LAW

shall continue to exist throughout Ireland until
further order.

*Given at His Majesty's Castle of Dublin,
this 26th day of May, 1916.*

RICHD. R. CHERRY, L.C.J.
J. O. WYLIE

GOD SAVE THE KING

Above: *Barricade erected in Lord Chancellor's Office by the rebels. Central Catholic Library.* **Below**: *German cartridges for a Mauser rifle found after the Rising — direct evidence of help from 'our gallant allies overseas'. Central Catholic Library.*

Above: *British soldiers mounting a checkpoint on the cordon around the city centre. Central Catholic Library.* **Below**: *British soldiers behind barricades shooting back at rebel positions. Central Catholic Library*

Pearse and Connolly (on stretcher) facing the failure of the Rising; the interior of GPO during the last days of the Rising. Painting by Walter Paget. Courtesy Pearse Museum.

Left: *Window in house at Mount Street Bridge shattered by bullets. Central Catholic Library.*

Below: *The ruined heart of the city: the statue of Daniel O'Connell, apostle of moral force, surveys the effects of physical force. Central Catholic Library.*

Above: *Eden Quay after the fire which was caused by shells from the* Helga, *the gunboat moored in the lower Liffey. Central Catholic Library.*

Below: *Loyal Irish Volunteers, who opposed the Rising, on guard duty in the city centre to prevent looting after the surrender. Central Catholic Library.*

The GPO was on fire, and about to collapse; ammunition had almost run out; there was nothing to be gained by further resistance. But the leaders felt that they had proved their determination. They hoped they had made the point that Ireland was a separate nation and should be given its own place in the peace-talks that would follow the world war. They had lit the flame of rebellion for their own generation.

Miss MacMahon came from the GPO with messages, and gave me a graphic description of what was happening there. She said, 'Mr Pearse would make you laugh; he was going around the GPO, like one in a dream, getting in the way of those trying to get things in order, and Mr Clarke said, "For God's sake will someone get that man an office and a desk, with paper and pens, and set him down to write".' There he sat writing most of the week, and brought out the paper called *The War News....*

On Tuesday, the lovely weather continued. Early in the day, a Post Office official who was a neighbour called to tell me that he had overheard a message, sent over a private wire at the telephone exchange, to the effect that an airship was being sent over that night to drop incendiary bombs on the GPO. Could I have word sent to the GPO? Miss MacMahon arrived early with messages, and I sent her back to the GPO with the message about the airship and the bombs. The GPO was darkened that night.

When Miss MacMahon had gone, I went into the garden to continue my planting. The ground was very dry, so I had a can of water to water in the plants. I had just laid it down when I heard a hiss, which gave me a shock. I fell over on my face and was unable to rise for some time. I did not know what the hiss was, but I examined the watering-can as soon as I was able and found two bullet-holes in it, one on each side. Where they came from I have never been able to find out.

KATHLEEN CLARKE, *Revolutionary Woman*

Dublin in ruins: Henry Street, looking westward from Nelson's Pillar.
Photograph T.J. Westropp, courtesy Royal Irish Academy.

Aftermath

As in so many of Ireland's rebellions, the reaction to it had more far-reaching effects than the event itself. Tried by court-martial, fifteen of the leaders of the Easter Rising were executed immediately, and Roger Casement some time later. Public sympathy had not been with the rebels to any extent, but now began to veer around. The executions seemed cold-blooded and vengeful, not serving any practical purpose but to create martyrs.

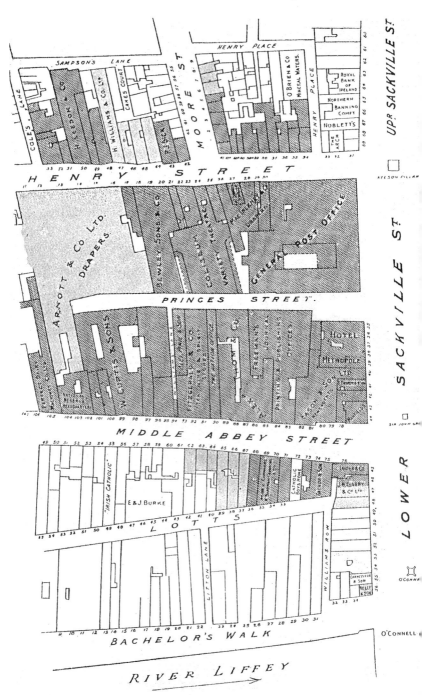

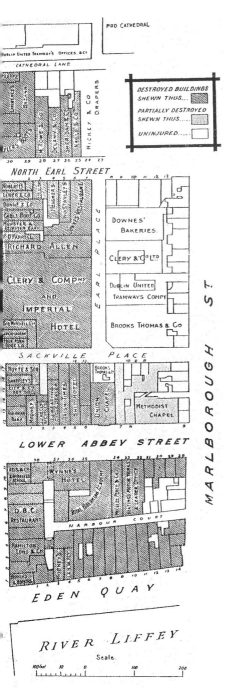

Map of areas of inner city destroyed during the Rising. Sinn Fein Revolt Illustrated.

Casement on trial for his life in London — the only 1916 trial held in public. National Library photo.

The mass of rebel prisoners were sent to prison camps in England. Most of them had been released by 1918, but in the meantime they had received proper military training and discipline, and been bound more closely to the Irish Volunteers (soon to become the Irish Republican Army). Irish republicanism now operated under the banner of Sinn Féin, as the British had mistakenly interpreted the rebellion as a 'Sinn Féin' activity. Griffith and other Sinn Féin members began to make political moves towards independence.

As British public opinion forced the government to engage with the Irish problem again, a War of Independence was waged from 1919 to 1921, until a truce was established. Britain's prime

The 1916 memorial in the GPO by Oliver Sheppard.
Courtesy Peter Costello.

minister, David Lloyd George, engaged in negotiations with Sinn Féin leaders such as Eamon de Valera and Michael Collins, who had both seen action in 1916. An Anglo–Irish Treaty was signed at the end of 1921, which gave Ireland not Home Rule, but something beyond that.

It was still not quite the Republic that generations had fought for, and Ulster had been partitioned from the rest of the country under Unionist pressure, but the leaders of the 1916 Rising might well have felt that their ultimate achievement was greater than that of any rebels of previous generations.

I assume I am speaking to Englishmen who value their own freedom, and who profess to be fighting for the freedom of Belgium and Serbia. Believe that we too love freedom and desire it. To us it is more desirable than anything else in the world. If you strike us down now we shall rise again and renew the fight. You cannot conquer Ireland; you cannot extinguish the Irish passion for freedom; if our deed has not been sufficient to win freedom then our children will win it by a better deed.

PATRICK PEARSE
Court-martial speech

EPILOGUE

The history of rebellion in Ireland since 1798 is that of a variety of causes — religious freedom, freedom from taxes or tithes, the right to vote, tenant right, an independent parliament — which all ultimately came together and focused on a republican nationalism. Ireland would be free, and would run her own affairs without princes or kings, with absolute equality and emancipation for all. Once Britain had been driven out, all else would follow. This was the dream.

Following the thread of these rebellions, it is notable how one seemed to follow from another, no matter how many years had passed between. Each generation left a speech or a watchword or a martyr, which could be passed on down to encourage passion and idealism. How much of this passion was wasted, this idealism corrupted by violence and hate?

Another aspect is the extent to which most of these uprisings were led by devotees who knew little about the people they professed to lead. They talked to one another, or to their committed followers, but never seemed to realise how the mass of the population saw them, or would react to them. More often than not, their dreams dissolved in incompetent failure, and it was the aftermath, rather than the event itself, that inspired other Irish men and women to follow where they had led.

Economic factors played a large role too. Land-hunger and penniless insecurity were potent forces to harness for a cause. But often the people were so racked by poverty and deprivation that they were unable to summon up the energy to respond to a clarion call, or else they were in reasonably secure conditions, and unwilling to rock the boat. The status quo must often have seemed more reliable, however unromantic, than the uncharted seas of some kind of republican revolutionary state.

Myth becomes more important than reality. Certain individuals stand out, and are remembered in song and story, often with little or no relation to the truth. But the masses are usually forgotten — the nameless camp-followers of the 1798 rebels who found themselves abandoned on cold hillsides as angry troops arrived to seek vengeance, Emmet's servant who refused to betray him and suffered for the rest of her life, the bewildered Dublin citizens who found themselves in the middle of a firefight in 1916. Were any of these rebellions really worth all the suffering they caused? Would Ireland have been worse off without them?

Let no man dare, when I am dead, to charge me with dishonour; let no man taint my memory by believing that I could be engaged in any cause but my country's liberty and independence. The proclamation of the provisional government speaks my views. No inference can be tortured from it to countenance barbarity or debasement. I would not have submitted to a foreign oppression for the same reason that I would have resisted tyranny at home.

...My lord, you are impatient for the sacrifice. The blood you seek is not congealed by the artificial terror which surrounds your victim; it circulates warmly and unruffled through its channels, and in a little time it will cry to heaven. Be yet patient! I have but a few words more to say. My ministry is ended. I am going to my cold and silent grave; my lamp of life is nearly extinguished. I have parted from everything that was dear to me in this life for my country's cause, and abandoned another idol I adored in my heart, the object of my affections. My race is run. The grave opens to receive me, and I sink into its bosom. I am ready to die. I have not been allowed to vindicate my character. I have but one request to ask at my departure from this world. It is the charity of its silence.

Let no man write my epitaph; for as no man who knows my motives now dares vindicate them, let not prejudice or ignorance asperse them. Let them rest in obscurity and peace. Let my memory be left in oblivion and my tomb remain un-inscribed, until other times and other men can do justice to my character. When my country takes her place among the nations of the earth, then and not till then, let my epitaph be written. I have done.

ROBERT EMMET, Speech from the Dock

BIBLIOGRAPHY

1798

Bardon, Jonathan, *A History of Ulster*, Blackstaff Press, Belfast, 1992.

Caulfield, J. (ed.), *The Mss and Correspondence of James, First Earl of Charlemont*, London, 1891–4.

Chart, D.A. (ed.), *The Drennan Letters*, Belfast, 1931.

Cloney, Thomas, *A Personal Narrative of Transactions in Wexford, 1798*, Dublin, 1832.

Croker, T. Crofton, *Popular Songs Illustrative of the French Invasion of Ireland*, London, 1845–7.

Dickson, D., Keogh, D. and Whelan, K. (eds.), *The United Irishmen: Republicanism, Radicalism and Rebellion*, Lilliput Press, Dublin, 1993.

Freyer, G. (ed.), *Bishop Stock's 'Narrative' of the Year of the French: 1798*, Irish Humanities Centre, Ballina, 1982.

Gahan, Daniel, *The People's Rising, Wexford 1798*, Gill and Macmillan, Dublin, 1995.

Gordon, Rev. James, *History of the Rebellion in Ireland in the Year 1798*, London and Dublin, 1803.

Hay, Edward, *History of the Insurrection of 1798*, Dublin, 1842.

Killen, John (ed.), *The Decade of the United Irishmen: Contemporary Accounts*, 1791–1801, Blackstaff Press, Belfast, 1997.

Lenihan, Maurice, *History of Limerick*, 1866 (republished Mercier Press, Cork, 1992).

MacDermot, Frank, *Theobald Wolfe Tone*, Macmillan, 1939 (republished Anvil Books, Dublin, 1968.)

MacNeven, W.J. and Emmet, T.A., *Pieces of Irish History*, New York, 1807.

Murphy, John A. (ed.), *The French Are in The Bay, The Expedition to Bantry Bay 1796*, Mercier Press, Cork, 1997.

Pakenham, Thomas, *The Year of Liberty*, Hodder & Stoughton, 1969.

Stewart, A.T.Q., *The Summer Soldiers: The 1798 Rebellion in Antrim and Down*, Blackstaff Press, Belfast, 1995.

Stock, J., *A Narrative of What Passed at Killala*, London, 1801.

Tone, W.T.W., *Life of Theobald Wolfe Tone*, Washington, 1826.

1803

Finegan, J. (ed.), *Anne Devlin Jail Journal*, Dublin, 1992.

Hume, G. and Malcomson, A., *Robert Emmet — The Insurrection of 1803*, Belfast, 1976.

Landreth, Helen, *The Pursuit of Robert Emmet*, Dublin, 1949.

McDowell, R.B. (ed.), *Memoirs of Myles Byrne*, Shannon, 1972.

Ó Broin, Leon, *The Unfortunate Mr Robert Emmet*, Dublin, 1958.

1848

Fitzgerald, Fr P., *Personal Recollections of the Insurrection at Ballingarry in July 1848*, Dublin, 1862.

Gwynn, Denis, *Young Ireland*, Cork, 1948.

Mitchel, John, *Jail Journal*, Gill, Dublin, 1921.

Moody, T.W., *Thomas Davis*, Dublin, 1945.

Murphy, Ignatius, *The Diocese of Killaloe 1800–1850*, Four Courts Press, Dublin, 1992.

1867

Clarke, Thomas, *Glimpses of an Irish Felon's Prison Life*, Maunsel & Roberts, 1922.

Comerford, R.V., *The Fenians in Context: Irish Politics and Society, 1848–82*, Wolfhound Press, 1985.

D'Arcy, William, *The Fenian Movement in the United States*, Washington, 1947.

Ó Broin, Leon, *Revolutionary Underground, The Story of the Irish Republican Brotherhood, 1858–1924*, Dublin, 1976.

Rose, Paul, *The Manchester Martyrs, A Fenian Tragedy*, Lawrence & Wishart, 1970.

Ryan, Desmond, *The Fenian Chief*, Dublin, 1967.

Ryan, Desmond and O'Brien, William (eds.), *Devoy's Post Bag* (2 vols.), Dublin, 1948 and 1953.

Ryan, Mark, *Fenian Memories*, Dublin, 1945.

1916

Brennan-Whitmore, W.J., *Dublin Burning: The Easter Rising from Behind the Barricades*, Gill and Macmillan, Dublin, 1996.

Clarke, Kathleen, *Revolutionary Woman*, O'Brien Press, Dublin, 1991.

de Paor, Liam, *On the Easter Proclamation and Other Declarations*, Four Courts Press, Dublin, 1997.

Edwards, Ruth Dudley, *Patrick Pearse, The Triumph of Failure*, London, 1977.

Haverty, Anne, *Constance Markievicz, an Independent Life*, London, 1988.

Le Roux, L.N., *Tom Clarke and the Irish Freedom Movement*, Talbot Press, 1936.

MacEntee, Seán, *Episode at Easter*, Gill, Dublin, 1966.

McHugh, Roger (ed.), *Dublin 1916*, Arlington Books, 1966.

Norman, Diana, *Terrible Beauty, A Life of Constance Markievicz*, Hodder & Stoughton, 1987.

Ryan, Desmond, *The Rising, The Complete Story of Easter Week*, Dublin, 1949.

Stephens, James, *The Insurrection in Dublin*, Macmillan, 1916.

Taillon, Ruth, *How History Was Made: The Women of 1916*, Beyond the Pale, 1996.

Ward, Margaret, *Maud Gonne: Ireland's Joan of Arc*, Pandora, 1990.

General

Boyce, D. *Nationalism in Ireland*, Gill and Macmillan, Dublin, 1982.

Bull, Philip, *Land, Politics and Nationalism*, Gill and Macmillan, Dublin, 1996.

Crossman, Virginia, *Politics, Law & Order in 19th-Century Ireland*, Gill and Macmillan, Dublin, 1996.

Dangerfield, George, *The Damnable Question, A Study in Anglo–Irish Relations*, Constable, London, 1977.

Doheny, Michael, *The Felon's Track*, Ed. Arthur Griffith, Dublin, 1914

Garvin, Tom, *The Evolution of Irish Nationalist Politics*, Gill and Macmillan, Dublin, 1981.

Kee, Robert, *The Green Flag: A History of Irish Nationalism*, Weidenfield & Nicholson, 1972.

MacDonagh, Oliver, *States of Mind: Two Centuries of Anglo–Irish Conflict, 1780–1980*, Allen & Unwin, London, 1983.

Madden, Dr Richard R., *The United Irishmen*, London, 1842–46.

Maxwell, William Hamilton, *History of the Irish Rebellion of 1798*, London, 1845.

Moody, T.W. (ed.), *Nationality and the Pursuit of National Independence*, Appletree, Belfast, 1978.

Orpen, Sir William, *Stories of Old Ireland and Myself*, London, 1924.

Sullivan, A.M. et al. *Speeches from the Dock*, Dublin, 1867.

Vaughan, W.E. (ed.), *A New History of Ireland V: Ireland Under the Union I, 1801–70*, Oxford, 1989.

Vaughan, W.E. (ed.) *A New History of Ireland VI: Ireland Under the Union II, 1870–1921*, Oxford, 1996.

Zimmerman, G.-D, *Songs of Irish Rebellion: Political Street Ballads and Rebel Songs, 1780–1900*, Dublin, 1967.

Index